TO THE URBAN FAMILY,
LIFE IS GOOD AND GOOD
THINGS DO HAPPEN!
WE LOVE HAVING YOU AS OUR
NEIGHBORS.
ERIC

# Eat the Damn Carrot

ERIC HODIES

Disclaimer: This book is based upon my own experiences, consultations with doctors and other health providers, and research. It is not a substitute for consulting with your own doctor. My hope is that this book motivates you to further your research and to make the best choices based upon due diligence and your unique situation.

ISBN-10: 0615742211
ISBN-13: 978-0615742212

# DEDICATION

To my amazing wife Carol, an angel who lives here on earth. I simply would not be alive, if not for you. You took care of everything. I love you so much.

And to everyone searching for their own cure.

# CHAPTERS

# ACKNOWLEDGMENTS

I was never alone on my journey. It was a team effort involving family, friends, neighbors, medical professionals, and the people I never met, blood donors. Whether you did something for me or just said something to me, it made a difference. And I will always remember you for it.

I am grateful for the nurses, doctors, and medical staff who have cared for me over the last 10 years. Some I only knew for a few minutes before a shot or a procedure, but still plenty of time to help me relax or tell a joke. Others have become lasting friends. Even the smallest compassionate gesture made my day better.

A special thanks to the nurses and staff of Fast Track at Beach General. My luckiest day was when I landed in your unit. On each visit, you impressed me with your skill, compassion, and humor.

I would like to extend my sincerest thanks to:
Blood donors, who give up precious time and a piece of themselves to save lives. I am here today because of your generosity.

My friends at the Blood Bank in Beach General, who carefully processed and provided my nearly 800 units of blood. You treated me like I was the only patient in the world.

Wendy Woolley, who spent many hours editing and contributing to this book. Every chapter has benefited from your insights and suggestions. Your encouragement has been invaluable.

Dr. Burt Alexander, my hematologist, friend, and contributor to this book. We were pilot and copilot on this amazing journey, and every appointment began with a big bear hug.

Ruth Harris, who spent countless hours keeping me company during my blood transfusions. I always felt better with you sitting beside me.

Ellen Ruddock, whose daily support, encouragement, and enduring friendship always brightened my day. Transfusion days weren't so bad when I knew that afterwards I would play and have fun with your son Evan.

John McLaughlin and all my friends from LANTDIV, who accommodated my illness and donated their precious vacation time so I could remain at work.

Beth Watson, for her invaluable help with the interior and exterior layout of the book. I would still be lost, if not for you.

Cori Fugal for creating original and imaginative cover artwork.

Martha Shurts, my sister-in-law, who always had faith things would work out for me.

Ann Tatlock, my sister-in-law, for lending her professional expertise to the editing of this book.

My brother, who I can trust to be where and when I need him. We were partners-in-crime making great childhood memories. Thank-you for your skillful cover photography and for writing a Foreword that came from the heart. And it's because of you that I have a title for my book.

My mom and dad, who believed in me and raised me to be able to deal with anything in life, including aplastic anemia. My dad had it tougher than anyone: No father should have to see his son fight for his life. My mom, in a fairy tale like story, introduced me to Carol, just a few weeks before she passed away. This is for you, Mom.

All those who have prayed for me or wished me well.

ERIC HODIES

# FOREWORD

At the 2005 Stanford commencement speech, Steve Jobs commented that when you reflect on your life, the various, seemingly unconnected dots line up in a perfect arc of reason and purpose. Jobs stated, "You cannot connect the dots looking forward; you can only connect the dots looking backward."

I am going to tell you about one of those dots in my brother's life.

My brother and I tried various organized sports such as baseball, basketball, and football, but ultimately we both lost interest, as we lacked the natural eye-hand coordination to excel in those sports. The desire to be athletic was innate though, and likely fueled by watching the 1972 Summer Olympics on TV and seeing our dad run.

Our dad began running in 1970, basically at the inception of the running boom. As kids, each evening we piled into the station wagon and headed for the high school where we attempted to keep up with our dad on the quarter mile cinder track. At first, we ran only a lap or two before ending up in the long jump sand pit where we challenged each other to leaping contests. However, my brother soon became more serious and started running almost every day. It was at this point that he began tracking his miles in a logbook.

If you ask Eric to show you his running logbooks, he will bring out about thirty or so pencil-filled journals identifying the course that day, the distance, how he felt, split times, and the weather. Each journal contains one year's worth of running entries, and it is quite an impressive compilation. As you flip through the many pages, you will quickly come to a startling conclusion: My brother rarely got sick or ever took a day off. He once had a streak of over 365 days of running. He even ran the morning after a tonsillectomy despite doctor's and parent's orders.

After college, Eric took up triathlons. I competed with him in his very first one: the inaugural 1983 Virginia Beach Sandman triathlon. I skipped more races than I competed in, but Eric raced in the Sandman every year. In fact, at the 20th Sandman triathlon, he was honored as one of only seven triathletes who had competed in all twenty races. Eric was the youngest of these seven, and I knew he would prevail in the end as the last of the seven to break the streak. Only a major illness would have stopped him, and sadly that is exactly what ended three decades of running and racing.

People often point to Arnold Schwarzenegger or Lance Armstrong as examples of individuals who were goal oriented with a single-minded pursuit. I put my brother right up there. The only thing he was missing was the raw natural talent to set records and make headlines.

My brother may be too close to the problem to see the solution, but I attribute his success to surviving aplastic anemia largely due to his focus and dedication to maintaining his health and researching the disease. That laser focus and steadfast dedication was cultivated and nurtured by his experience in trying to become the best runner and triathlete he could become. Only when I look back at Eric's life do I see that dot--the cumulative effort of hard work and intensity which ultimately helped save his life.

No matter your particular view on Lance Armstrong's character and his recent admission about doping in his Tour de France career, a lot of hard work went into being an elite, professional cyclist. A favorite commercial of my brother's was a Nike sponsored anti-doping advertisement back in 2001 where Lance voices over "Everybody wants to know what I am on?" After some video of Lance working out, sleeping, lab testing, he responds, "What am I on? I'm on my bike, busting my ass 6 hours a day. What are you on?"

Eric would answer the question of what am I on slightly differently. "I'm eating the damn carrot, that's what I'm on"

So how did the phrase *Eat the Damn Carrot* come about? The first time I heard my brother use it was to chastise me for catching the common cold for the umpteenth time. Never mind that I have kids or that (according to current research) I may just have a more sensitive allergic reaction to the symptoms of the common cold, my brother came to his forthright conclusion that I was not taking care of myself properly. "Get more sleep!" he would urge. "Drink more water!" Finally, he would end his advice with the exclamation, "Just eat the damn carrot!"

In other words, quit looking for the easy way out, and instead, eat simple, nourishing foods. Rather than relying on vitamin and mineral supplements, he told me to get the nutrition directly from the whole food. The closer your food resembles the form found in nature, the stronger the health benefit you will receive. Eventually this mantra took an even broader form of definition. The advice goes well beyond eating fruits and vegetables. It is about getting back to basics by exercising, maintaining a positive attitude, getting educated on your disease process, and becoming your own advocate.

By the time you are finished reading this book, you will be well acquainted with each of these tenets that fall under my brother's mantra. Along the way, you will be amused, saddened, touched, motivated, and inspired by his experiences and turn of events that all began in 2002 when he was 41 years old.

Now, it would be a disservice to the readers of this book if I did not share the nature of the relationship I have had with Eric over the years. When I was a teenager, my brother made threats to my life a daily routine and so a natural distance occurred between us during that time, as I was blazing my own path in life. But with time and experience comes maturity and perspective. I have come to realize that my brother has been a positive constant force in my life, providing encouragement and support during good times and bad. He continues to push me competitively, reminds me to eat healthy, and advocates for me to follow a better family-work balance.

If you had asked me ten years ago whether I thought my brother would still be with me today, I would have said no. After a period of shock once his diagnosis was confirmed, I started to mentally prepare myself for his passing. As is typical for most people with busy lives, I had never seriously stopped to think about what life would be like without him until I was confronted with this cruel and premature eventuality that his illness was forcing me to face. Talk about a wake-up call!

I now look up to my brother more than I ever thought possible, and admittedly his health challenges are partially to credit. He leads his life with an amazing calmness and appreciation, which brings a zest for living that I aspire to as well. His laser-like clarity of what is truly important for happiness is an inspiration to everyone he meets. And with that clarity comes an honesty that has brought us even closer as brothers. Great relationships are so important in life, and the older I become, the more I realize how fortunate I am to call Eric not only family, but friend.

So, as you are reading this, if you recognize that you have someone who would be truly missed if they were suddenly taken from your life, there is no better time than now to reach out, say Hello, and renew your efforts to keep in touch. Appreciating what is here and now is a valuable lesson for all of us.

- Marc Hodies, his younger (bigger) brother

# CHAPTER 1 ~ BEATING THE ODDS

*Doctor: I have some bad news and some very bad news.*
*Patient: Well, might as well give me the bad news first.*
*Doctor: The lab called with your test results. They said you*
*have 24 hours to live.*
*Patient: 24 HOURS! That's terrible! What could be*
*WORSE? What's the very bad news?*
*Doctor: I've been trying to reach you since yesterday.*

*Source: Unknown*

"I beat the odds." For 10 years, I have dreamed of saying those words. Now I can.

When I was in the best health and fitness condition of my life, I was diagnosed with aplastic anemia, a very rare autoimmune disease of the bone marrow that results in critically low levels of blood cells. Without a response to a treatment, I was given about two years to live, that is, if I was one of the fortunate ones who didn't succumb to an infection or a hemorrhage within the two year period. Well...that was 10 years ago.

Today I have undergone a spontaneous partial remission and my bone marrow is miraculously making blood cells again. My port catheter has been removed ending a decade of weekly blood transfusions. I have survived critically low blood counts, chemo treatments, a brain hemorrhage, iron overload, and countless drug side effects. People have asked me, "How did you do it?" Well, I am here to tell you the answer is "I Ate the Damn Carrot." (See the Foreword for the origin of that phrase.)

So what does it mean when I say I ate the damn carrot? It means I took a holistic approach to living and went back to the fundamentals of life by filling my mind, body and soul with nutrient rich, empowering sources of energy. Everything I consumed, literally and figuratively, had a purpose. It was to make me a smarter, stronger, and happier patient, in order to maximize my ability to fight my disease and beat the odds.

My remission wasn't found in a new drug or a special food or in some kind of miracle pill. And although I consider my cure a miracle and give credit to my higher power, it wasn't granted to me by just praying to God for countless hours while I lay in a hospital bed living out my diagnosis. My miracle was a result of being an active participant in my cure, not by accepting any pre-determined prognosis.

For 10 years, I had to leave behind my pre-illness life that was more than 40 years in the making. I lost my health, but I also lost my job and the ability to do some of the things that previously brought me great satisfaction. Instead of daily workouts lasting an hour or more, I traded that for a short walk or a little yoga. Instead of mowing the lawn once a week, I traded that for one day a week in the hospital. Previously, I had never been on a prescription drug, but I traded that for watching units of donated blood from strangers drip into me.

My life was turned upside down. But I had a plan to get through it. I wasn't sure if I was going to live or die, but my plan gave me something to grab onto and hang my hat on. I couldn't see the light at the end of the tunnel, but I knew every tunnel has a light at the end of it. And I was going to try my hardest to get to it.

My plan allowed me to channel my energies into something real and practical. Instead of sitting idly by, I was engaged and working on my cure. Every time I went for a walk or had a nutritious meal, I was working on my cure. Every time I sat at the computer and educated myself, I was working on my cure. And every time I shared a laugh with a friend, I was working on my cure. I felt like I had found an edge in beating this disease. Even in my low points, I stuck to my plan. It worked!

This book is about my commitment to healthy living, which I promote as being the secret behind my success. How you choose to live your life, with or without an illness, can ultimately determine your fate. Though my recovery can be called a "miracle," I believe that if others follow the principles in my plan, more people would experience similar positive outcomes. I've met too many patients who were not educating themselves, not eating well, not staying active, and not staying positive. Too many of them are not around anymore.

Taking action will empower you and leave you with a sense that anything is possible. Setbacks are inevitable, but when you have a plan of action, you will always have that feeling that you can help yourself. Use this book to spur you to create your personal plan of action. And if you are not ill at present, don't wait to hear your diagnosis before incorporating key principles into your daily life. Begin today.

In the following pages, I detail the changes I made and the actions I took that gave me the best chance for living. These are common sense methods, not some new and controversial treatments, and they cost nothing. They are not guaranteed to miraculously cure you or even to restore your health. But they are guaranteed to give you better odds of returning to health. Or staying healthy if you are not now sick. These are methods that have been proven to work and have been borne out by scientific research. Everyone, healthy or sick, should be living these principles.

Don't live out your diagnosis. Your doctor may describe the most likely path and outcome for your disease, but you're always free to take action and blaze your own trail. Many patients don't know there are options beyond conventional medical treatment that can be very effective. Your mind and body are capable of amazing things, and they are under your control. What you do outside of the hospital walls can be just as important as what you do inside those walls.

My hope is to inspire you to make changes to become a more active participant in your care even if the changes you make aren't exactly the same as the ones I made. My aim is for you to take ownership of your illness, become your own advocate, and to be part of your own cure.

The time to act is now. Your body is your greatest and most valuable asset and what you put into it and how you treat it can ultimately determine how many years you get out of it. Make a few easy changes and start down the path to better overall health. I hope this book helps to start you on that process with practical steps to improve your health. You owe it to yourself.

# CHAPTER 2 ~ MY STORY

*"The ultimate measure of a man is not where he stands in moments of comfort and convenience, but where he stands at times of challenge and controversy."*

*- Martin Luther King*

On September 15th, 2002, I ran full speed into the Atlantic Ocean along with 750 other triathletes for the 20th annual Sandman Triathlon held in my hometown of Virginia Beach. I was 41 years old, and I swam, biked and ran in every Sandman since the race began two decades ago. Only six other participants in the race that day could make the same claim. Jumping into the ocean surf and racing in the Sandman at the end of every summer felt so natural; I was sure I would always compete in it.

Following that triathlon, I ran some road races during

October and November of that year, but with increasingly disappointing results. I was familiar with fatigue, but this felt like I was running with the proverbial bear on my back. I had turned 40 just the year before, so at first I just chalked it up to getting older. My friends had a few good laughs saying I was "over the hill," but I had hardly been sick a day in my life, so I never suspected anything serious. Instead, I did what every recreational athlete does after turning in a bad performance: I tried to train harder. But I knew my body, and my symptoms became more difficult to attribute to age.

By December I was getting short of breath just walking across a parking lot. I swallowed my pride and saw my family physician, who prescribed an inhaler for what he believed to be asthma. A couple of weeks later, when I didn't show any signs of improvement, the same physician took a blood sample to check my labs. My results came back on Christmas Eve. My wife, Carol, who is a nurse, received the call that would change my life.

My blood counts showed alarmingly low levels of white cells and red cells. My platelet count, the body's ability to clot, was at the panic level. The nurse also told Carol that an appointment was scheduled for me to see a hematologist the following week. What my doctor didn't know was that we were leaving the next morning to visit Carol's dad in

Asheville, NC, where I had stubbornly planned to run/walk/crawl up Mt. Pisgah. (It had always been a fun challenge to see how fast I could go up the steep trail to the summit at 5721 feet.) With blood counts as critical as mine, running up the mountain might have been fatal. It scares me to think how everything might have worked out differently, if my results had come back just one day later.

Instead of a holiday family vacation, we headed for the hospital. Doctor's offices were all closed, and Carol was concerned that in case this was acute leukemia, a day or two could make a significant difference in my prognosis. When we first entered the emergency room, we were told we could not be admitted for "low blood counts." We began to walk out, but then we turned around and tried again, this time focusing on my symptom of shortness of breath. I was taken to the ER right away.

This was my first lesson, of many lessons, on the importance of being your own advocate. No one will argue that the medical system is hard to navigate. The many safeguards in place so that hospitals, doctors, and insurance companies do not get abused will occasionally result in angry and frustrated patients. If you are sick long enough, it's inevitable you will encounter obstacles along the way. These obstacles will appear without warning and will seem insurmountable. It's important to be insistent, ask lots of questions, and always pack your patience.

In the ER, I underwent several tests including numerous blood tests, a chest x-ray, and an EKG. I was also put on oxygen. Once those test results came back, I was admitted as a patient. The EKG revealed cardiomyopathy (enlarged heart), and an abnormal rhythm. In one hour, I went from arguing my way into the ER to becoming an in-patient with several major health issues. (Fortunately, the enlarged heart was later explained as an athlete's heart.) It was Christmas Eve, and that was the end of any testing or evaluating for another day and a half.

In retrospect, I consider that first night in the hospital the beginning of an amazing journey that would take 10 years to complete. The journey would also change my life forever. On that night, I began learning much about a world I previously knew very little about. I learned that disease does not recognize holidays like Christmas and does not care about past achievements in athletics. Disease is the proverbial "bull in the china shop." It will change you and your life, whether you like it or not.

I learned that hospitals are places where you can have the pleasure of meeting extraordinary people one minute, and the next minute be talking to someone who has absolutely no interest in you. Hospitals are drab and monotonous, and the food is the same. Inside hospital corridors, machines beep endlessly, windows never open, food is delivered at scheduled times, patients are poked and prodded, and you are identified by the numbers on your plastic wrist bracelet. It all felt a little too much like a prison or a zoo.

My neighbor once told me she would stare for hours at a bus stop she could see from her hospital window. She would watch people get on and off the buses and remember what it felt like to have that freedom to go where she wanted whenever she wanted. It's not until we get sick that we realize how much of life is taken for granted.

As if that is not enough, in a hospital you are issued those wonderful backless gowns that are worn whether you are having a procedure performed, walking down the corridor, eating a meal, or visiting with friends. As I sat in my hospital bed that night, I thought it would be only a day or two before a doctor would fix me up and send me back home to go running again. I had no idea of what lay before me and how much my life was about to change.

On the day after Christmas, I had my first bone marrow biopsy. I was placed flat on my stomach with my rear end exposed to the world. A four inch needle (I swear it looked over a foot long!) was manually pushed through the skin until it met the posterior iliac crest. (The iliac crest is the most prominent bone in the pelvis and you can feel the tip of it by pushing your hands into the side of your waist.)  At that point, the doctor twisted the needle to advance it through the bone and into the marrow, where a sample was retrieved.  Although the numbing medicine made it tolerable, it served as a good introduction to the hundreds of needles that would be stuck into me over the next ten years.

The bone marrow is where stem cells produce the blood cells that circulate through our body. Unfortunately, my biopsy revealed a bone marrow almost completely devoid of stem cells and replaced by fat.  My diseased bone marrow was known as "aplastic," literally translated as "without form."  The disease I had, aplastic anemia, is very rare and potentially fatal.  The cause was idiopathic, which means there is no known cause.

With an empty bone marrow, I was missing three critical components found in blood that are essential to live.  I did not have enough platelets, white cells or red cells.  Without white cells, I had no immune system to fight off germs.  Without red cells, my body could not get enough oxygen to my brain and other vital organs.  And without platelets, my blood lost the ability to clot, and a simple cut or trauma would be serious.

After four days, I was released from the hospital.  I was on oxygen my entire stay, and I felt like it had become a bit of a crutch or a safety net.  I was headed home, but I had become weaker, not stronger. And though I now had a diagnosis, I left with even more questions than when I arrived. The next step was to talk with my hematologist and decide upon a course of treatment. Until then I would require weekly red cell and platelet transfusions to stay alive.

I went through a number of adjustments that first week after my hospital stay. I had to adapt to a hemoglobin (around 8.0 g/dL) that was only half of what I had lived with my previous 41 years. Hence, normal daily activities weren't always so normal and sometimes humorously so. For instance, near the end of every meal, I'd get so overwhelmingly tired, I'd just slide out of my chair and take a 10 minute nap right on the kitchen floor. I tried to fight it, but I simply didn't have enough blood to digest my meal and stay awake. Our dog Greta, who was also fatigued from her treatments for lymphoma, welcomed her new napping buddy.

One evening we invited my dad over for dinner. I was enjoying a beer while we waited for him to arrive. When the doorbell rang, I got up to get the door. Only I never made it that far. I passed out after just a few steps. This was frightening to Carol, as my aplastic anemia diagnosis was still so new, and she wasn't sure what to expect. Carol called 911, and because the local rescue squad was busy, the fire department was dispatched. I regained consciousness just before four fully outfitted fire fighters walked into our living room.

The firefighters took my vitals and asked me my name, what day it was, and a few other questions. It became apparent to everyone in the room (including me) that it was the combination of anemia and alcohol that had caused me to lose consciousness. At that point, one of the firefighters asked me what kind of beer I had consumed. When I proudly replied that it was a Guinness Extra Stout, he said it was well worth it and everyone had a good laugh. They put me on a stretcher and took me to the ER to get fully checked out, and that was the end of my Guinness beer drinking for a long time.

Approximately two weeks after my diagnosis, I chose horse Anti-Thymocyte Globulin (ATG) for my treatment. It is a type of chemotherapy that acts as an immune suppressant on the lymphocytes, and it is generally considered the standard first course of treatment for most aplastic anemia patients. The idea is to suppress my own autoimmune response that has somehow gone haywire, and then allow it to gradually come back to normal. I began the four-day infusion of ATG in January 2003 at the University of Virginia Hospital in Charlottesville, Virginia.

I tolerated the chemo at first, but by the third day, I developed serum sickness and had uncontrollable chills, fever, and diarrhea. I was as sick as a dog. The bathroom was four steps (I counted them) away from my hospital bed, but it might as well been a mile. I was having a world class bout of diarrhea, and one particular night I spent so much time on the toilet I thought it would make more sense to just move my bed into the bathroom. Fortunately, I started feeling much better (and lighter) in a couple of days. Though I left the hospital as not a big fan of ATG side effects, it was overshadowed by the fact that I was absolutely sure the treatment was going to work.

If I responded positively to the ATG treatment, I would likely see a rise in my blood counts within a few weeks and almost certainly within 90 days. I was getting twice weekly blood counts, and as the weeks passed by without even a slight rise in counts, I grew restless.

I literally held my breath every time my doctor passed the lab report to me. Inevitably, all my blood counts flagged with double exclamations and my platelet counts were designated with the letter "P" for panic level. My doctor wrote a script for a blood transfusion, then I spent the rest of the day in the hospital, and that cycle repeated the following week. I honestly couldn't understand it. I thought someone else might be a non-responder, but not me.

The photo on the previous page was taken on a particularly trying day, as I came to grips with having failed my first chemotherapy treatment.

Being pro-active, my doctor, Carol, and I explored other treatments well before the 90 days had expired. We made trips to VCU Medical Center and Johns Hopkins Hospital to see hematologists. Our task was simplified by the fact that there were very limited options available to individuals, such as myself, who do not respond to the initial ATG treatment. My options were to retry the ATG again, undergo a bone marrow transplant, or enroll in a phase II clinical trial using a very highly toxic chemotherapy. When my only brother tested negative as a match for a transplant, the decision was made easy.

We decided on a clinical trial at Johns Hopkins which used high dose cyclophosphamide. It was a very rigorous experimental treatment using the strongest immune suppressant known to man. As my doctor said at the time, "It's a control-alt-delete reboot for the human body."

The rationale for using high dose cyclophosphamide is to kill every blood cell in the body so there is no memory of the programmed immune attack against the bone marrow. It is the ultimate weapon against an autoimmune attack, but it carries significant risk. Without white cells, I would be left completely vulnerable to all types of bacterial, viral, and fungal infections. While the bone marrow underwent the reboot, I would have to wear a respirator mask at all times except while eating and sleeping.

Some people get cyclophosphamide as chemotherapy for cancer, but my treatment was many times stronger than that dose and extremely toxic. It was only a Phase III study so there wasn't much data, but we thought it looked very promising.

My doctor sat down with Carol and me and reviewed the buffet of potential side effects (including death) that I might expect from a course of high dose cyclophosphamide. But that wasn't the way I heard it. Whenever he said the word chemotherapy or cyclophosphamide, I only heard the word cure. Why would I be afraid of that? I was sure something this powerful would work perfectly. I phoned and e-mailed my doctor almost daily, asking when I could come in and start on my cure.

At the same time we received word on which date I was to begin, we also received a letter that was completely unexpected. My insurance company reviewed the proposed treatment and decided not to authorize it. I was stunned. I couldn't fathom how a necessary medical treatment could be denied. They did not provide an alternative treatment, just some words about disqualifying the treatment and a big fat "Treatment Denied" in the box labeled "Determination."

It was mind numbing and it made me angrier than I had ever been in my life. I'm surprised I didn't have a heart attack. It was the insurance company, not my doctor, who was making decisions on the care I could receive. In essence, without their medical approval, they were telling me that they would only approve blood transfusions. Did they know my medical situation better than my doctor? Transfusions were just a short-lived solution. Without additional treatment, I would die.

Of course, this happens every day, regardless of which insurance company you have. It's just the nature of the beast, and I had similar occurrences several more times over the years. But that was little consolation. They were robbing me of my chance to live. I imagined someone sitting in a cubicle, without any medical background, stamping "Denied" because it cost too much. Forget about having a desired patient outcome or saving a life, it was all about the company's bottom line. I was livid.

It's particularly sad because the added stress, for a chronically ill person, is detrimental to their already frail health. My doctor, accustomed to seeing insurance company denials, tried to calm me down and say there was a good chance he could change the determination. He and his staff made phone calls, filled out extra insurance forms, and provided additional medical history information. Ultimately, this resulted in the decision being reversed and a lesson learned. If you want something bad enough, you have to fight for it. Do not take no for an answer, especially when your life depends on it.

On June 29, 2003, we arrived in Baltimore where we were to live for the next two months, assuming there were no complications. We were instructed to rent an apartment as close to Johns Hopkins as possible. After the in-patient stay for the chemo treatment, I was required to commute to outpatient appointments, twice a day / 7 days a week for a minimum of eight weeks. We were also instructed not to choose an apartment near any type of construction because disturbing the earth would likely release germs that would be harmful to me.

After we moved in, Carol cleaned our apartment like my life depended on it, which it did. When she was done, it was the cleanest apartment in Baltimore. Without an immune system, this would be my safe house. Besides my hospital room and the out-patient areas of the hospital, it was the only place I would see for the next eight weeks. No one, not even my family, was allowed to step foot into our apartment. When fresh flowers arrived from friends, we put them outside on the balcony. I lived like I was the boy in the bubble.

On June 30, 2003, I started three days of medical appointments and testing. I had blood work, respiratory testing, lung scans, transfusions, and doctor appointments. I also had a central line (a Hickman catheter) surgically inserted into my superior vena cava (large vein that empties into the heart) to simplify the administration of chemo and transfusions.

It took awhile to get used to the 12 inches of tubing dangling outside my chest, but the Hickman catheter made life so much more bearable, as it saved me from hundreds and hundreds of peripheral venous sticks over the years. To keep the line from clotting, I had to flush it with saline and heparin syringes every day, without fail. I would end up flushing that catheter thousands of times.

Though I enjoyed my catheter, it made taking a shower difficult. The gauze pad over the site had to stay dry or the moisture would become a breeding ground for germs. Carol came up with an ingenious plan where I folded a wash cloth and taped it over the site. This would absorb any moisture. Then I stuffed the tubing in a plastic sandwich bag and taped the bag to my chest over the wash cloth. Even then, I was always careful not to stand directly under the water.

Every Sunday, Carol and I would clear our kitchen counter and transform it into a hospital bed. I would climb onto the counter and lay face up, as Carol would proceed to put her mask on. Using medical supplies from our home health company, we would change out the aforementioned dressing. We took great pains to make it a sterile procedure, as infections of the catheter can be very difficult to eliminate. And if the dressing got wet or sweaty, we would change it out during the week, too. We did this without fail, every week for more than 9 years. In all that time, I never once had a catheter infection. All in all, the absence of needles was a great benefit, and my catheter became my best friend.

Finally, my treatment day arrived. Two nurses dressed in full protective gear, including face shields, very carefully brought in the bag of cyclophosphamide. The word "BIOHAZARD" was plastered across it in large letters along with some other ominous warnings. If that was supposed to make me nervous, it didn't work. I wasn't trying to act tough. I just figured the bag contains medicine, the medicine cures me, and I go back to having fun. It all seemed pretty straight forward to me.

I asked if they could hurry things up and start dripping the chemo into me. I joked with them that I was in a hurry because I had to get back to training for my next Sandman Triathlon. After some more kidding around, they asked me if I was at all nervous. Of course I was a little nervous, but more than anything, I just wanted to get cured as soon as possible.

I received four days of the chemo and although I didn't feel my usual chipper self, I never experienced nausea, fever, organ failure or any of the other possible side effects. The last morning in the hospital, the rounding doctors entered my room, but I wasn't there. I was down the hall on the treadmill. A nurse brought me back to my room and I apologized for holding them up. I will never forget the look on their faces. They did not typically find their chemo patients on the treadmill after treatment. I knew I was lucky to have done so well, but I have to give a lot of credit to my previous healthy lifestyle, positive outlook, and Carol's great nursing care.

The chemo worked as advertised and a few days later, all my blood counts plummeted. I clearly remember the first time the lab results came back and the number next to WBC (white blood cell) was zero. Nada, none, zilch. Normally I would have around 7000 cells per microliter, but now I did not have a single white cell in my body.

It was a strange feeling, walking around knowing I was completely defenseless. I wore my mask at all times (except in our apartment), but it was little consolation. If we walked down the hospital hallway and heard someone ahead sneeze, we would turn around, make a mad dash down the hallway, rush down the stairs to another floor, and wait five minutes before returning.

Since we were in a hospital with a lot of sick people, we did our "escape from the germs" dash quite often. I'm sure our reaction looked comical, but we didn't laugh much. That sneeze may as well have been the black plague to me. Even if I was lucky, it would be months before I would have any immune system of my own. Prophylactically, I was put on several antibiotics and antifungals.

The second effect of the chemo was to make my hair fall out, at first in bits, then in big clumps. I sped up the process with a razor and then took a look at the strange guy gazing back at me in the mirror. There's a bit of trepidation when you find out if all that hair has been covering a funny-shaped head all your life. I immediately started liking my new "do" and told everyone I would keep it shaved until I was better again. Ten years later, I like my low maintenance hairstyle too much to let it grow back.

Every day (and occasionally twice a day), Carol and I drove from our apartment in the Baltimore suburbs to the hospital for blood work, transfusions, and doctor visits. Each morning, we waited with anticipation of the results of my blood counts. I grew accustomed to seeing the number zero next to WBC.

Finally one day, the lab found a few white cells under the microscope. Several days later, the number of cells was high enough to be picked up by the machine. Over the next few weeks, the numbers slowly increased.

Two months after my chemo, my white blood count had increased enough that I was finally allowed to take off my mask. It was a huge relief. Though I'm not sure how much protection the mask really offered, I initially felt very vulnerable without it. I was still severely immune-compromised, but it was now safe for me to return home. It was August 23, 2003 and I remember everything about that trip, as if it was yesterday.

I had just finished two months of hardcore treatment, and I could practically feel my body healing. I was bursting with hope and anticipation. I remember crossing the Chesapeake Bay Bridge from Annapolis to the Delmarva Peninsula. When I saw dozens of sailboats crisscrossing the Bay, I thought I'll soon be able to go sailing again, if I want to. I'll soon be able to do anything I choose.

The chemo had wiped my bone marrow of all blood cells, and now we waited for normal levels to return, minus the autoimmune attack. For some lucky people the process takes only a few months, for others a year or so, and for others it never happens.

On October 12, 2003, a little more than a month after returning home, the 21st annual Sandman Triathlon was held. The treatment had not increased my blood counts and I was still receiving weekly red cell and platelet transfusions. When the race director heard that my streak of 21 races in a row was in jeopardy, he made a one-time exception to the rules and allowed me to participate as part of a relay team. Friends would race the swim and bike legs for me, while Carol and I would walk the three mile run. In addition, donations were accepted to further research in aplastic anemia.

The race director presented me with the "# 1" racing bib and publicly recognized me before the start of the race. I was overwhelmed. Since I received my most recent transfusion just two days prior, I was able to do a rough imitation of a jog when I was about 100 yards from the finish line. I smiled as my catheter tube bounced around on my chest. I had to hold back tears of joy, as the crowd loudly cheered for me at the finish line. The Virginian-Pilot, our local newspaper, sent a features writer and photographer to cover the story and the next day it was in the paper. (Article reprinted with permission in the Appendix.)

Months passed and my blood counts didn't budge as a result of the cyclophosphamide treatment. I stayed on supportive care through the use of weekly blood transfusions. My platelet count was almost nonexistent (usually around 2,000 when normal is 140,000 - 400,000) and bleeding was a continuous problem. As a result, I always had plenty of petechiae (spontaneous capillary bleeding) dotting my skin. Just brushing my teeth led to oozing gums, and it was not unusual to awake to a bloody pillow case.

These gum bleeds wouldn't clot for hours or even a day or two. We bought some QR blood cut powder, the same substance the military uses to stop bleeding in the field. I don't believe it was meant for internal use, but I was losing precious red cells through the constant bleeding and I was embarrassed to go out in public with a bloody mouth. The powder worked for the most part, and I was able to hide the bleeding from my friends and family.

Living with an extremely low platelet count was like walking on egg shells. It easily caused me the most worry, as any kind of trauma could cause internal bleeding, and a simple fall could result in a deadly hemorrhage. A friend I had corresponded with lost her eyesight because of a bleed. Then in June of 2005, I had the event all aplastic anemia patients dread.

While visiting with my brother and his family on the beach, I developed a pounding headache. The next day the headache persisted and my gait became unsteady. At first I attributed these symptoms to side effects from a medication I was taking. Then I developed numbness in my face, left arm, and left foot. I should have never ignored these symptoms.

We rushed to the hospital. I was put on morphine for the headache, and given a CT scan. The scan revealed a hemorrhagic stroke in the cerebellum portion of my brain. It was a miracle that I did not bleed until my brain filled with blood. Though I was aware of the gravity of the situation, it was months before it really sank in. Among aplastic anemia patients, a brain hemorrhage is a major cause of death, second only to infection.

When the bleeding had stopped, the clot in my brain measured 12 mm in diameter. It left part of my body numb and it gave me a monster headache that had me hitting the morphine pump often. But what gave us all pause was trying to understand why my gum bleeds would take forever to clot, but my body found a way to stop this particular clot, in my brain of all places. Someone was looking over me.

I spent one day in the intensive care unit and then was transferred to a regular room. Three days later, I left the hospital with a cane and a limp. When I returned home, I resumed my neighborhood walks, forcing my body to build new neural pathways. Within a week, I had no need for the cane. I felt like the proverbial cat with nine lives, and I just used one up.

Residual numbness continued to disappear even a year after the stroke, which is somewhat rare. At present, the only reminder of my hemorrhage is a bit of numbness in my left hand, left foot and left side of my face.

Though it was a miracle that I did not bleed out, my brain hemorrhage was a low point. Needing blood transfusions was one thing, but the stroke was a message, received loud and clear, on just how sick and vulnerable I was. It had been over two years since my diagnosis and I wasn't going anywhere, except to the hospital for weekly blood transfusions. I was getting increasingly tired of the whole process and my prognosis was not good.

Up to this time, I was still employed as a mechanical engineer. My supervisor and my co-workers had been amazingly accommodating, as I was missing a day or two per week for doctor appointments and transfusions. I also worked from home, but I preferred the office environment. Though tiring, I felt like a normal person in the office, and it was greatly therapeutic. But after my stroke, Carol and I reevaluated the value of work.

We had many difficult conversations about life, death, finances, and emotions. In the end, we decided the time was right for me to leave. I told everybody that it was important for my health that I was well rested. All my energies would be better spent on activities that would keep me strong for whatever I might face in the future. And though I rarely spoke of it, I also knew that my disease would likely prove fatal. My brain hemorrhage was evidence of that. I enjoyed life too much to chance working to my final day.

I wasn't surprised at how hard I cried when I informed my supervisor I was leaving. I told myself that I was leaving my career behind in order to put all my energies into getting better. But a large part of me felt like leaving work was just code for "I'm giving up and going home to face the inevitable." I had no earthly idea if I was making the right decision, but it made the most sense at the time.

After wrestling with these issues, the time seemed right to have a "Celebration of Life" party. In case something happened to me, I wanted to show my friends how much their support meant to me. It was an amazing day. (More on this party in Chapter 7)

An unfortunate side effect of my repeated red cell transfusions was the accumulation of excessive iron. As red cells reach their life expectancy, they die and leave behind iron. In a healthy bone marrow, new red cells are formed using the iron left from the dead red cells. And since the human body is unable to eliminate iron, repeated transfusions can lead to dangerous and even lethal levels of iron. In order to reverse the build-up of iron, I was prescribed Desferal (deferoxamine), a very expensive iron chelating drug.

A bag of the medicine and a pump were enclosed in a fanny pack that I wore for 14 hours a day six days a week. The drug entered via my port catheter, chelated the iron as it circulated through my body, and was eliminated in my urine, which always had a reddish-rust color.

I couldn't help but hear the whirring noises from my pump as it injected the Desferal all night and a good part of the day. There was no escaping it. To make matters worse, I didn't tolerate the drug very well. I developed double vision, ringing in the ears and neuropathy (nerve damage) in my arms and legs. Though most people regain previous vision and hearing upon discontinuation of the drug, there were no guarantees.

For someone who had always treated his body as his temple, it really hurt to abuse it this way. These side effects were a lot to handle. I accepted aplastic anemia, but keeping my vision and hearing was non-negotiable.

I remember trying to watch TV. The picture was blurry, the sound was muddled, and I couldn't enjoy it because my legs would not stop tingling. This really had me on edge. The dose of the medication was lowered and then lowered again. I also infused the drug over 16 hours, thus giving my body two extra hours a day to metabolize the medication. I didn't like wearing the pump for 14 hours a day, and I liked

16 hours a day even less.

However, after several months of waiting, the symptoms gradually subsided. Unfortunately, at the lowered dose, I was eliminating iron only a very modest amount faster than I was accumulating it. This continued for years and it was an irritating inconvenience, as even a shower had to be scheduled around my chelation therapy. Finally, in November of 2005, I heard some amazing news. The FDA had approved Exjade (deferasirox), a new iron chelating drug, to be taken orally.

My days (and years) spent tethered to an infusion pump were about to end. I felt like I had just won the lottery. And thanks to my persistent nagging (of my doctor and insurance company), I was one of the first in the country to start on Exjade on December 9, 2005. I loved my new freedom. I tolerated the new medicine well, and for the first time, I was eliminating the iron at a significantly higher rate than I was accumulating it. I had just used another one of my nine lives.

The weekly platelet and red cell transfusions continued, most without any problems. Occasionally I would get a few hives in reaction to the platelets, but 50 mg. of Benadryl usually took care of the problem. On two occasions, the reaction was serious enough to force the platelet transfusion to stop. Then on December 3, 2007, I had an anaphylactic reaction.

I happened to be up and walking around the unit when everything turned dark and voices seemed far away. Seconds later I lost consciousness and dropped to the floor. Everything happened so fast, there wasn't even time to yell for help. A code was called over the hospital PA system and by the time I awoke several minutes later (thanks to an injection of Solu-Cortef), there was a crowd of people surrounding me. There were several nurses, a doctor, a respiratory technician, and Carol, who by chance happened to be walking down the same hallway seconds after I passed out. After a recovery in the ER, I was able to go home. Yet another crisis averted.

In early March 2008, I suddenly felt more out of breath and fatigued than usual. Just a day after getting two units of red cells, I was completely worn out again. My hemoglobin sank to all time lows and I had to receive transfusions twice a week. Yet, I still didn't have the energy to do anything except sit on the couch all day. Carol recognized my hands had the mottled appearance of someone who was dying. It was the weekend, but the look on Carol's face told me we were on our way to the hospital.

Through blood tests, my hematologist Dr. Burt Alexander quickly diagnosed it as Coombs-positive hemolytic anemia. It was another autoimmune attack. It took a little while to wrap my head around two concurrent autoimmune attacks. How did I get so lucky?

This one caused my red cells (the few ▪
own plus the cells I was getting in transਛ▪
stack up like a roll of coins, rendering them useless.
The descriptive term for how the red cells stack up is
called Rouleaux, which seems like a very elegant name
for such an unpleasant condition. I was prescribed
antibiotics and steroids to blunt the autoimmune
attack. Fortunately, I responded well, and I began
feeling better in just a few days. Once again, I felt like
the proverbial cat with nine lives, and I just used
another one. I wondered how many more of those
lives I had left.

For years I continued to receive frequent transfusions
of donated red cells and platelets. I remember
thinking back to when I received my first unit of
blood, I didn't even consider the possibility I would
see unit number two. Then I thought maybe I'll have
to put up with a dozen or so units before a treatment
would kick this autoimmune attack. But here I was,
getting one unit after another and passing major
milestones....400 units, 500 units, 600 units. As luck
would have it, my blood type is AB positive or the
universal acceptor, which means that my blood is
compatible with all blood types.

Each year the Red Cross ran into a shortage of blood,
particularly around the holidays, but I never fretted.
If there was a shortage, I would be given whatever
blood type was in the greatest supply. In addition,

any possibility of mistyping the blood products (extremely remote) did not concern me.

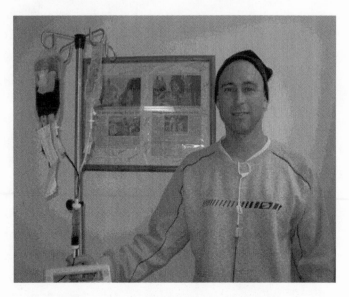

*Getting transfused with one of my 800 units of blood.*

As the years wore on, I would have done nearly anything to make the endless transfusions, medications, and doctor visits stop. I was generally happy and was able to get out and enjoy life. I had even adjusted to the riskiness of my life, but I had lost a good deal of my previous identity. It had been 8 years since I saw those boats in the Chesapeake Bay, but I had yet to go sailing. I wanted to do more and it bothered me.

I often wondered how long someone could receive weekly blood transfusions. There had to be a limit.

Every therapy had a risk and so did the blood transfusions. Unfortunately, there weren't any other conventional treatments or therapies available for a non-responder, such as myself. After hundreds of units of transfused blood, my body had built up so many antibodies that a non sibling mismatched bone marrow transplant would have almost no chance.

Meanwhile, I had a decent quality of life living off of the blood transfusions. Dr. Alexander said many times that I was doing a remarkable job "walking the tightrope" between health and illness. We decided I would not try any treatments at all, and I would accept my current quality of life and live like that for as long as possible. I felt like doing "nothing" was, in fact, doing something. I was making a bold move that would determine how I would live the rest of my life. It was the toughest decision I made over the ten years.

The amount of time I spent in the hospital, without any real hope of ever getting better, would change anyone. Living on this tightrope, I felt like I was looking at life through a pair of binoculars with everything just a little more in focus than before. I had a different perspective on life. I discovered that the list of truly important things in life is very, very short. Everyone knows that, but you really feel it deep inside of you when you're in that hospital room. Also, the little things in life really are little. (Well, except for bad drivers, who I think will forever remain irritating)

Before my illness, I ran an occasional road race, usually spending a few minutes commiserating with my friends about our nagging injuries. A little ache or pain that could keep one from running for a few weeks seemed like a big deal. I'm almost embarrassed to say I sometimes took part in that kind of talk. The world of hospitals, chemotherapy, and funerals of friends of whom I had met during transfusions changed all that.

I watched how disease changed others and how disease had changed me. My philosophy had always been to do my own thing for my own reasons and not be concerned with what others were doing. I applied this philosophy to all aspects of my life, but this disease tested that way of thinking.

Everyone diagnosed with a disease must travel their own path. I had been on my path, deciding when to turn left, turn right, stop, and go. But after so many years without a cure, I began second guessing my strategy. Why were others cured, but not me? Was I doing enough, or did I miss something? Should I try that exotic herb that is sold online as a miracle cure? I was spending a lot of time wondering if I had turned over every stone in a search for my cure. I can tell you it's a lonely and futile exercise that only results in making your head spin in circles.

Since the very first day of my illness, I kept a detailed log book of all transfusions, medications and lab results. I knew my blood counts and chemistries in my sleep. For eight years, my platelet count had always been 5k or less (normal is 150k-400k). In early 2011, one of my labs came back with a 6k platelet count. I just assumed the machine was out of calibration or maybe it was feeling a little generous with the numbers that day.

A few weeks later I had a 7k platelet count. My white count had also ticked up an insignificant amount. I remember the day my platelets were 8k because I could not take my eyes off the number 8. Clinically there is no difference in those numbers, but I began to look forward to getting my blood counts.

It was early 2011 and all of my counts had inexplicably started to rise, and the interval between blood transfusions lengthened. It was an insignificant improvement at first, just a little bump in counts and a day or two more between transfusions. The increase in blood counts was steady, but painfully slow. It was several more months before it amounted to anything significant. Eventually I was going several weeks between transfusions.

At first it seemed like a dream. I had always hoped to get better, but I lived with realistic expectations. It had been eight years since any kind of treatment, and there was no apparent reason for this remission. I wasn't on any medications, not even vitamins. I tried to stay calm, and I held back telling others the news until I was absolutely sure my counts were rising.

The blood counts continued to rise, but at a snail's pace. After months and months of anticipation, it finally became too much to ignore. Ten years after the immune attack from hell, my bone marrow was waking up and producing blood cells. They were far from normal amounts, but enough. I was free of transfusions! This wasn't a dream. I was getting a second chance. Life was suddenly full of possibilities.

Unrelated to any previous medical treatment, my bone marrow was waking up from the autoimmune attack and undergoing a partial spontaneous remission. For the bone marrow to recover from such a sustained and difficult attack was a miracle.

As 2011 rolled into 2012, I was able to begin working out again. All my counts were still low, but that hardly mattered to me. My red cell count was anemic (around 11 g/dL), but that was higher than it had been in almost 10 years. I was feeling better and eager to get back to running. On my daily walks, I started to do the occasional slow jog from one street light to another. Gradually, I felt stronger. I lengthened it to two street lights and then to the length of a block.

On April 17, 2012, we felt confident enough about

my remission that I had my central line port su
removed from my chest.  Although my platelet count
had improved, it was still too low for any kind of
surgery, so I had to be transfused with one unit of
platelets.  It would be my very last unit of red cells or
platelets.  And for the first time in more than nine
years, I did not have a medical device buried in my
chest.

About a month after the operation, I accomplished
what I could have only dreamed of just a few months
prior.  I put on running shorts and went over to the
high school track, where I had competed more than
30 years ago.  I ran a single slow lap (a quarter mile)
and stopped.  With the completion of that one lap, I
had summited my own Mount Everest.  I took a seat
up in the bleachers and stared out into space.  I
thought about how much fun it was to run that lap,
and I thought about everything that led up to that
moment.  I thought about how blessed I was and how
lucky I was.

It was a couple of weeks later when I ran two laps
without stopping.  I immediately rushed out to the
store and bought a pair of running shoes.  I was back!

By June, I had worked my way up to one mile.  I was
as slow as a turtle, but that didn't matter.  I signed up
to do my first race, the Allen Stone Memorial Race
5K (3.1 miles) held on the Virginia Beach boardwalk
and scheduled for July 21, 2012.  My goal was to

simply run about a mile or so, and then run/walk the rest of it. Only that wasn't exactly as it happened.

For years I had cheered on my best friend and her family at the Allen Stone race. This year they would be pulling for me. With that encouragement and with Carol running alongside of me for most of the last mile, I felt like I was being pushed along. I ran down the boardwalk on emotion, not physical ability. I was running towards health, leaving the chemo, blood transfusions, and hospital rooms behind me. It was magical and it was spiritual. If someone had described a run in those terms before that day, I would have just smiled. Now, I understood. My disease had changed me. I knew this was a moment to cherish forever.

Amazingly, I didn't stop running until I crossed the finish line. My pace was slow and I didn't bother to look at the clock as I finished. It was completely irrelevant. I finished 11th out of 12 runners in my age group, but I wouldn't have been any happier if I had finished in first place. This race was not about time, but about the life I wanted to get back. The finish line didn't merely mark the end of a 5k race. I felt like Dorothy reaching Oz after her arduous journey down the Yellow Brick Road. I had found my finish line at the end of a long, bumpy road that took me where I had never been, taught me things I never knew, and made me into a different person.

# CHAPTER 3 ~ KNOWLEDGE IS POWER

*"Depend on the rabbit's foot if you will, but remember it didn't work for the rabbit."*

*- R. E. Shay, humorist*

When I was first diagnosed with aplastic anemia, I wouldn't have known a red cell, a white cell or a platelet if one hit me square in the head. Autoimmune disease? Bone marrow failure? I knew next to nothing of those. And why would I? I was about as healthy as one could be, rarely getting the common cold, much less a chronic illness. I would worry about that some other time.

The world of hospitals, doctors, health insurance, and chemotherapies were also subjects that were unfamiliar to me. Of course, I heard occasional medical stories through Carol, a nurse. I listened, but dismissed most of what I heard, on the basis that it could never happen to me. After I became ill, I learned an important lesson: No matter how much you may think you know, everything changes when you are thrown into it.

So I was clueless about anything and everything bone marrow related, but that ignorance didn't last long. I knew knowledge would be my ally in this fight to stay alive. From day one, I resolved to be proactive in understanding all that was happening. I would ask meaningful questions in order to get meaningful information in return. Only by being knowledgeable would it be possible to make informed decisions regarding the care of my body.

Becoming educated on your disease and disease process doesn't happen overnight. It's like learning a new skill or a foreign language. It takes some time and effort, but it's worth every second. And once you gain that knowledge, you will have added a very potent weapon in your fight to regain health.

When you understand the disease process and why some unpleasant things are happening to your body, the shock and surprise factors diminish. You know the possibilities beforehand. You may even feel like you have some control over what is happening. Most importantly, when you are informed, you are able to make better decisions that ultimately determine your overall outcome.

I'd be lying if I said that what I read online didn't occasionally rattle my nerves. That is a risk you take by fishing around the internet. Aplastic anemia is a very serious, potentially fatal disease, so comprehending the treatments and the mortality statistics was unsettling. It definitely did not make for happy bed-time reading. Initially, I didn't believe the "bad stuff" would happen to me: someone else maybe, but not me. So I shielded myself somewhat with that way of thinking. The best advice is to read up on your disease with a family member or friend sitting beside you. Things are always scarier when you're alone.

I am an engineer by trade, and I treated my illness as a design problem just waiting to be solved. But like any good engineering problem, I first had to gather all the known data. Only if I learned as much as possible about my "design problem," could I go about selecting the optimal solution.

I recognized I had to keep an open mind, while I listened and read everything I could get my hands on. My goal was to become as knowledgeable as possible, so as to understand as much of my disease process as possible. That meant scouring the internet, writing emails, and picking the brains of as many experts as possible. But unlike the engineering data I was accustomed to working with, medical information is not as black and white. Machines are predictable, but every patient is different, and predicting outcomes is part art and part science. Science is great, but sometimes very big decisions have to be made utilizing a healthy dose of intuition.

The internet was a great tool at the start of my education process. Of course, when you are dealing with a disease like aplastic anemia, which strikes only two people in a million, it takes a little more work to find information and experts. Diseases that are so rare are called "orphan diseases" because teaching hospitals and pharmaceutical companies are reluctant to expend great amounts of money to work on a potential cure for so few people. Alas, medicine is a business driven by money.

I found the best places to start my research was with teaching hospital websites and the charitable foundation that supports my disease. Teaching hospitals usually are at the forefront for research, innovative therapies, and clinical trials. They are where clinical trials are used to find new cures. They also have a strong commitment to education.

My two treatments were at teaching hospitals, and the morning rounds to my room usually included three to five doctors, plus physician assistants and nurses. For those few minutes in the morning, I had a captive audience focused solely on my case. Besides making me feel very important, it was encouraging to know such a considerable amount of brain power was deliberating on my case and offering input.

The Aplastic Anemia & MDS (myelodysplastic syndromes) International Foundation was an invaluable source of information on the bone marrow failure diseases. I gained an enormous amount of knowledge, downloaded seminars, checked for clinical trials, read journal articles, got in touch with others, and much more. They also put me in touch with others facing the same diagnosis. Hearing how others were coping gave me the feeling that I was not alone.

Journal articles, free of charge, can be found from a number of sources. The AA & MDS website (or whatever foundation supports your particular disease) has many articles available. Your doctor can usually accommodate your request. And lastly, you can e-mail the particular journal. I've registered to receive weekly e-mails from the journal "Blood" containing links to abstracts. When I see an article I'm interested in, I e-mail the contact at the journal and explain I am an aplastic anemia patient. My request has never been denied

As part of my education process, Carol and I sought out the expertise of four hematologists before selecting my first chemo treatment. It was exhausting, and it involved travel, hotels, and time off from work for Carol. But we never considered not doing it.

Notice I used the phrase "selecting my first chemo treatment," because in the end, this was my body and my choice. My doctor laid out the options, but this was my journey and I would choose the path we would take. For better or for worse, I was going to select the treatment for my body, for no one knows my body like I do. And I would be a better patient for taking an active part in my cure.

Amazingly, after visiting the four doctors, we were left with three different options. At least it was amazing to me. Shouldn't there have been more agreement between the doctors? What is a patient to do when confronted with different treatment options? Which doctor is right? One, all, or none?

It was a real dilemma, and it gave us plenty to think about. I have to admit, it was times like this, when I was a little jealous of the folks who would seek the medical opinion of just one physician, assume it was their only option, and go on their merry way. It certainly was an easy, low stress way to go. I undoubtedly dug deeper and got more involved with my disease and my care than I needed to. I did it by choice. And I believe it played a major role in why I am alive today.

Two doctors will offer different treatment choices because in the end, doctors are just like the rest of us: naturally optimistic or pessimistic, inclined or averse to risk, and influenced by practicing in their particular hospital or group practice. They have likes and dislikes just like their patients. And as I discovered, the treatment of choice can even be a political decision, driven by the hospital's administration.

This is a great place to put a plug in for the movie "Lorenzo's Oil." One of my doctors suggested I watch it, when he noticed my thirst for information. It's based on the true story of a family searching for a treatment for their son, who has a very rare debilitating disease. The parents undertook a relentless search for knowledge and a cure for their son, but the harsh realities of that process are heartbreaking.

The four doctors who we consulted all made compelling arguments for their choice of treatment. The doctors were very educated, highly trained, and well regarded in their field. These were the experts, and as we listened to them, we hung on every word they said and jotted down notes as fast as possible. All the treatments recommended had at least some success. However, there were many other variables to compare, such as severity of side effects and mortality, which made it a little like comparing apples to oranges.

I remember my brother saying my dilemma was like asking someone to make you a chair. The carpenter will suggest wood, the ironsmith will suggest metal and the craftsman will suggest wicker. Of course, everyone's opinion is influenced by their background. However, this was my health, not a chair.

One hematologist advised me to undergo a particular form of chemo that another hematologist would not even consider using because of its toxicity. A second doctor would not treat with the first doctor's treatment of choice because of its lack of durability. The third hematologist advised me to have an unmatched bone marrow transplant and we were proudly shown around the unit where I would have the transplant. There was even a kitchen dedicated to transplant patients. I was in need of a cure and this looked like my ticket back to health.

This doctor showed us mortality and survivor rates for transplants and made a compelling argument for a complete and durable cure. A bone marrow transplant was tempting. However, I had built up antibodies as a result of my many transfusions and these would be a liability during a bone marrow transplant. In addition, my only brother was not a match.

Even in the case of perfect matches, graft versus host disease, a common side effect of bone marrow transplants, can be devastating. The donor's immune system can attack the host's body, including the eyes, skin, intestines, and lungs. And that's even if you survive the procedure. A young, strong surfer, who I met through my transfusions, chose the transplant and died of a massive infection during the procedure. In the end, I felt like an unrelated donor transplant would be too risky.

This was my wake-up call that medical statistics can be misleading. There are survival rates and other data available for various treatments, but there is no way to report or graph the oh-so-important quality of life. Months later, while I was in the bone marrow failure unit at Johns Hopkins, I started talking to those around me. Some of these patients had undergone transplants months or even years earlier. For reporting purposes, they were "successes" and that was great. But graft versus host disease had left some looking like burn victims, others suffering from chronic nausea and vomiting, and others downing daily cocktails of 20 meds or more.

Cure rates on a website or a piece of paper are one thing, but seeing those "cured" patients in person in the unit was entirely different. According to the trial protocol, these patients, who were alive a specific number of years post-transplant, had undergone successful treatments. However, the cure rates on paper did nothing to portray the patient's quality of life. It was eye opening. At this point in my journey, I was still hopeful for a different kind of success.

Success rates are even harder to determine with clinical trials. Clinical trials are how new medicines are approved and brought into practice. The government's NIH website has all the trials listed, along with answers to almost every question. My treatment at Johns Hopkins was a phase II study. (There are 4 phases to trials.) I was only the 41$^{st}$ patient to enroll in the study, so there wasn't much information on success rates to base our decision on.

I had already learned from my previous treatment that success is highly subjective. On paper, success rates for a treatment will vary from 1% to 99%. That's of limited help in making a decision. As a patient, any treatment I chose would be either a 100% success or a 100% failure. Carol and I wanted to choose the best treatment based solely on sound logic and reasoning, but that only took us so far. In the end, all the medical data had to be put to the side and the decision had to feel right on an emotional level.

It's true, people spend more time choosing the television they watch or the car they drive than choosing the doctor who may determine if they live or die. What if you were going to put a new roof on your house? You'd probably interview more than one contractor in order to collect a couple of estimates. Isn't it worth the effort to find the right doctor for your needs? I still remember the exact moment, early on in my diagnosis, when my hematologist, Dr. Burt Alexander said, "This is a team effort, so I want your input. If you have another idea, let me know. You have the final say and I don't want you doing anything you don't feel is right." It was his job to send in the play, but ultimately it was up to me, the guy out on the field doing battle, to go with that play or call an audible. Keep searching until you find the doctor that makes you feel empowered.

Things really changed from that moment on. Not only did I not want to let myself down, I didn't want to let my doctor down either. When I became a partial owner of my cure, I grew energized and sensed I could tackle anything that came my way. I soaked up that responsibility. I didn't walk blindly into my doctor appointments. I studied my disease until I knew it inside and out. I researched therapies and drugs. I knew the side effects of the drugs I was taking. And I walked into my appointments with specific questions and follow-up questions based on what I was told. It doesn't matter if you have aplastic anemia, cancer or heart disease; know your disease. Take ownership of it.

Doctors also need some help from us, the patients. Dr. Alexander advises, first and foremost, that patients should always bring a friend or family member to all appointments. Besides the obvious emotional support, this person can provide an invaluable service as another set of ears and can jot down notes to read later. Many times, patients, upon hearing their diagnosis, will never hear another word after that.

Dr. Alexander encourages family involvement. He insists that those patients who have extensive family involvement are the ones who have better outcomes. The day I spoke to him about this chapter he told me he had just returned from walking into a patient's hospital room, only to find 15 friends and family crammed into the little room. I thought any doctor would be bothered by that. Dr. Alexander was overjoyed by the sight.

Dr. Alexander is pleased when there is a great deal of family involvement, but advises that just one person act as a spokesperson or historian for the patient. That person can send out an e-mail summary of appointments and lab work to friends and family. Patient to doctor e-mails can be very helpful, but they are legal documents, and sometimes things are best explained in the office visit. So use e-mails for short, simple questions or to give the doctor a heads up on what you would like to discuss at your next appointment.

Doctors love it when their patients are educated. Do your research and then ask questions. But be cautious about bringing in reams of paper as a result of printing out everything you've found on your disease. Appointment time goes by quick, and doctors usually have a number of items they are already planning to talk about. It's best to either drop off the papers at the office a few days in advance, ask the scheduler if you can add a block of time to your appointment or schedule another follow up appointment just to talk about your research.

Though there weren't any viable treatments available to me, I never gave up reading journal articles and e-mailing doctors around the world. Some countries approve treatments before the United States, and I wasn't going to discount any possibility, even if I needed to travel abroad. I received replies from doctors in Switzerland, Israel, Canada, and England, but sadly they could not offer any additional help. My friends thought I was doing a stellar job of accepting it all. But deep inside, I was desperate for a cure and would have eaten or swallowed nearly anything if it promised health. I would have gladly gone ten rounds with the meanest, biggest, most ornery crocodile, if it granted me a cure.

The temptation to do anything for a cure can lead one to Google searches of "miracle cures." I was no different and the results were amazing. Those two words will get you about 1.5 million hits. I guess anyone can have a miracle cure, as long as you have a credit card. When conventional medicine has not worked, it's so easy to fall into that trap. Alas, there are miracles, but no miracle cures. None of those cures that I found had been tested by the FDA and common sense said they would be either a waste of my money or possibly a danger to my already fragile health.

Years passed since I failed both chemotherapies. There were a couple of other therapies (e.g. steroids) that had very limited success, mostly with people who had experienced a partial response to a previous treatment. But I had been treated with the strongest immunosuppressant known to man without any results. As my doctor at Johns Hopkins, who prescribed my use of high dose cyclophosphamide to blunt the autoimmune attack, said, "Why would you try to use bullets to kill this thing, when you've already used cannonballs?"

By not pursuing any other potential therapy, I had a disease that I wasn't treating. Why would I do that and not try something, anything? It was a tough question and one that Carol and I wrestled with endlessly. It just felt wrong to not pursue some kind of treatment. Waiting around for a situation to improve on its own was not my usual way of handling a problem. Not in my personal life and not in my career. My proactive personality was all about solving problems. Besides, how many things in life actually get better by doing nothing?

We weighed the risks vs. benefits over and over and always came up with the same answer. I had gone through all the conventional treatments and anything else would have been speculative, with a high risk factor and little chance of improvement. Of course, doing nothing meant staying on supportive care with blood transfusions ad infinitum, which carried plenty of risks. Supportive care carried with it the assumption that death was not too far into the future. Though very sick and vulnerable, I had a decent quality of life that I did not want to risk giving up. It was one of the hardest decisions of my life. We chose to "do nothing" and it was mutual with Dr. Alexander. In hindsight, it probably was the decision that saved my life.

I was fortunate, because not treating a disease is rarely a viable option. And even when it is, it goes against our nature as doctors or patients. There is much controversy these days regarding the overuse of scans (prostate antigen assay, mammogram, etc.) and how they can lead to unnecessary biopsies and treatments. For example, many prostate cancers grow slow enough that they never need treatment. In the end, the "not treat" option worked for me, and it probably could be explored in other cases, too. My point isn't to tell everyone to skip treatment, but instead think outside the box, dig deeper than the statistics, and not follow some pre-determined path based upon your disease and likely outcomes.

My mantra, throughout my illness, was to learn as much as I could about everything, but sometimes, in spite of our best intentions and diligent research, the unexpected happens. For seven years, I had a Hickman port catheter in my chest to make chemo and blood transfusions easier. One end of my catheter sat in my superior vena cava, just outside the right atrium of my heart. This allowed the chemo drugs to be diluted by the bloodstream as quickly as possible. The rubber tube ran from the superior vena cava through my jugular vein, before exiting from my chest. Outside of my body, this tube ran for several inches before splitting at a Y. The two separate rubber lines each terminated with a connector valve for easy access. This allowed for more than one infusion to occur simultaneously.

After five years of heavy use, I started to wonder how long my catheter would last. I couldn't find a patient, nurse or doctor that knew of a Hickman catheter implanted for as long as mine. There were no visible signs of wear, but I was concerned, as I knew from mechanical engineering that materials eventually wear out and some parts prone to heavy cyclic use (like the Y in the tube) are susceptible to mechanical fatigue.

I set out to do my trademark thorough research by quizzing nurses, doctors, the home health care company sending me catheter supplies, and Bard, the catheter manufacturer. The answer was a unanimous "it can stay indefinitely." Most replies also included a "can't remember hearing of someone having a Hickman catheter implanted for so long."

I wasn't completely reassured by these answers, but what was I going to do? I could replace it, but that required two procedures, one to remove the old catheter and one to implant a new one. These were normally low risk procedures, but nothing was a given for someone with neutropenia (extremely low white cell count) and a next-to-nothing platelet count. Of course, if the catheter broke unexpectedly, it would be life threatening. Carol and I debated it for weeks, ultimately deciding to leave my catheter in place "indefinitely."

One day, about six months after making that decision, I noticed blood oozing out of the catheter at the Y, exactly where I had been concerned. My parents could be proud that the money they spent on my mechanical engineering degree had paid off, but that was of no help right now. Carol clamped the tube above the Y, and we went to the hospital. The Y was removed, and I was left with a single lumen Hickman catheter.

About a year after that, while watching TV one night, I looked down and saw my shirt soaked in blood. When I looked at my catheter, I saw the there was a split in the tube. The rubber had simply dry-rotted. I now had an opening straight from the largest vein in my body, and I was bleeding out at a high rate.

Carol thought quickly, raced to a desk drawer, and grabbed a couple of ordinary office butterfly clips to clamp off the tube upstream of the break. The bleeding stopped immediately. I changed out of my blood soaked shirt so as not to scare anybody in the ER, and we headed to the hospital.

After seven years, I finally had to say good-bye to my trusty Hickman catheter, but a few weeks later, on April 2<sup>nd</sup>, 2010 it was replaced with a power port catheter.

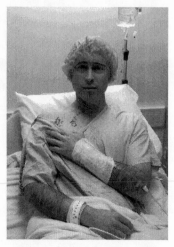

Afterwards, I realized just how lucky I was that my catheter broke while I was awake. If it had split an hour later, when I was asleep, I likely would have bled to death. I had the feeling that I just used up another one of my nine lives.

From the minute I was diagnosed, becoming educated on my disease and everything going on around me was my highest priority. I made the vow that I would be heavily involved in my care. And I would be an active participant in every appointment. Not everything went according to plan, and I had plenty of scary moments. But ten years later, I can look back and say my knowledge of bone marrow failure and its process has been a great asset. Always cognizant that any medical journey is full of unforeseen pitfalls, I knew I was as prepared as possible.

In 2002, I started out on my journey having never heard of my disease or knowing anything of blood cells. But by 2011, I was selected to sit on the Patient Education Council of the Aplastic Anemia and MDS Foundation. It was a nice recognition and now I'm one of several patients, doctors, and health care providers who advise and comment on future content for the Foundation's website and written materials. I sure have come a long way.

# CHAPTER 4 ~ THE MIND-BODY CONNECTION

*"Each patient carries his own doctor inside him."*
*- Norman Cousins, author of*
*'Anatomy of an Illness'*

Fast Track was the name of the unit in my local hospital where I received the bulk of my nearly 800 units of red cells and platelets. It was a small open room, about 30 feet by 15 feet, with 8 reclining "movie theater" type chairs placed around the perimeter of the room. There were curtains that could be pulled around each of the chairs, if needed for privacy. It was named Fast Track because patients who needed a dressing change or a shot or a round of antibiotics could get in and out quickly.

It was common knowledge that I spent my

transfusion day in chair number 8. I sat there the very first time I went to Fast Track and never even looked at another chair again. I was just like the guy who strolls into the local bar at the same time each week and sits at the same bar stool. I also had a standard cocktail order (two units of reds and one unit of platelets) that my bartender...uh, I mean my nurse...knew by heart. And instead of beer nuts or pretzels, I had all-you-can-eat saltines. What a deal!

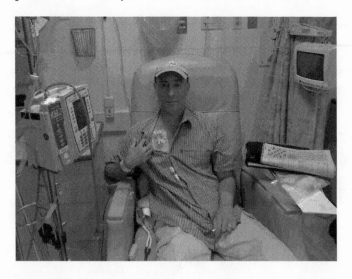

*Chair #8, where I sat for every transfusion.*

The nurses and staff in Fast Track were my friends, and they did everything possible to make my day easier. After years of transfusions, I knew nearly everybody on staff. If there was an equivalent of a tenured professor for patients, I was it. I would stroll around like I owned the place, and I was asked more than once by other patients if I worked in the unit. The nurses always got a good laugh out of that. I was most proud when the nurses framed the newspaper article of my 21$^{st}$ Sandman Triathlon, signed the matting, and hung it on the wall behind chair number 8. It always seemed to make my spot just a little bit more inviting, and I would not take it home until nine years later.

Though it was called Fast Track, blood transfusions were anything but fast. To safely introduce one unit of red cells into the body, it needs to be infused over two hours. Work in the time for patient registration, nurse assessment, more paper work, and a peripheral IV stick, and you've just tacked on another hour or more. If you're getting two units of reds and a unit of platelets, you need to count on a minimum of eight hours.

Because of the smallness of the room, the arrangement of the chairs, and the many hours spent there, it was almost inevitable that conversations with other patients would be initiated. Again, just like your local bar. Of course, not everyone wanted to talk, but many did. Others watched TV talk shows, read books and magazines, slept, or worked on their laptop. I was the curious sort and wanted to know more about the folks I was spending so much time with, so I was usually up for some conversation.

Sometimes we talked about what the weather might

be like (there were no windows in the room), our favorite sports teams (back to the bar analogy) or the bland hospital food (my favorite topic), but on occasion, it was serious talk about life and death. The gravity of those conversations was unlike any I have ever had outside the hospital, and the names and faces of those patients are etched into my memory. Sadly, I've been to the funerals of several of my fellow roommates.

When you go to your job, a ballgame or a restaurant, there is a common voluntary interest that brings everyone to that location. But in Fast Track, it was a melting pot of very different people, unlike other places you might frequent. Disease doesn't care who you are, your age, or your background. I met a well-known United States congressman, a restaurant owner, and an accomplished artist. We had only two things in common: We were all sick and none of us wanted to be there. Bonds of friendships were formed on that basis alone.

When the talk turned to diseases and chemos and such, it was easy to pay attention. I was naturally interested in what others were dealing with or what doctor they were seeing, so I asked lots of questions. But far too often, I would get blank stares when I asked someone what they were "getting" that day. Many times they had no clue whether it was a chemo, an antibiotic, or some other drug hanging in the bag above them. How could they not know? They were allowing some foreign substance to drop into them for hours on end. Did they choose not to know?

From my days as a cross-country runner, I knew that runners are basically broken down into two groups. There are those who associate (tune in) and those who dissociate (tune out). Dissociative thinkers refer to those runners who think about anything but running when they are putting in the miles. They're out there thinking about the pot roast cooking back home or when they have to pick up their kids from soccer practice. Thinking this way helps divert the fatigue of the workout, and most recreational runners fit into this category. The best runners practice associative thinking. They are constantly assessing their body, checking their legs, energy levels and thinking about the task at hand.

To cope with illness, there must be times of dissociative thinking. But if the best and fastest runners practice associative thinking, it makes sense that the patients, who are aware of what is happening to them and how they are feeling, will fare better because they are more in tune with their body.

Whether we are in tune with what is going on around us or not, the body and mind are constantly interacting. This interaction can occur positively or negatively, and with vast implications for a patient.

Experiments have shown that even short-term stressors affect the functioning of our immune system. Our T-cells actually look different depending on whether we are happy or not. If even one negative thought can damage our immune system, then we owe it to ourselves to do all we can to lower our levels of stress.

Stress is especially harsh on our cardiovascular health. It causes increases in blood pressure and cholesterol levels, which all raise the risk of cardiovascular disease. Stress also appears to play a role in inflammation, which is a key process in developing heart disease. Clearly, we need to free our mind of stress to the greatest extent possible.

Most people who get diagnosed with a disease eventually hear the classic story of how Norman Cousins dealt with his stress. Cousins, a professor and author, was getting discouraged by his health issues, when he came upon the idea of treating his stress with laughter. After watching Marx Brothers movies, he noticed he felt much better. Cousins said, "I made the joyous discovery that ten minutes of genuine belly laughter had an anesthetic effect and would give me at least two hours of pain-free sleep." And when the pain returned, he went back to watching his comedies.

I know my mindset going into my treatment at Johns Hopkins was one of the reasons I tolerated it so well.

The chemo was high dose cyclophosphamide, one of the most toxic therapies in medicine. Side effects can be very serious, and some weak patients die from the toxicity of the drug.

Right from the start, I assumed a drug that powerful acting on a body as healthy as mine (other than the aplastic anemia) was certain to be a cure. I wasn't being cavalier, and I wasn't trying to act tough. I certainly wasn't naïve about what was happening. In spite of the seriousness of the situation, getting cured just seemed like a reasonable and natural expectation. The heck with the cure rates, this chemo was my one way ticket back to health.

Author Carol Kuykendall employed a similar strategy. After a year of chemotherapy treatments to treat Stage IV ovarian cancer, she adopted a golden retriever puppy. When mulling over potential names, she decided on Kemo, because she wanted to see chemo as her friend. She said she planned on taking her dog to chemo centers to let others know, "Kemo is your friend."

We all have a bias and tendency to see certain things in everyday life which others many not notice. One person sees the chemo as a cure, and another sees only the severe side effects. This selectivity in attention is also why different people can sit in a doctor's office and hear the same diagnosis, but each one will remember it differently. This selectivity to pick out what we want to hear is called the "Cocktail Party Effect." In a noisy room of people and different conversations, most people can still hear if their name is spoken. No matter who was talking to me, I always heard the word "cure."

When the nurses came in to hang the first bag of chemo, they wore safety gear designed to protect them from the dangerous chemical, which was going to be infused straight into my bloodstream. I watched the nurses work and made a few jokes. They administered several medications to protect my internal organs from the toxic effects, which gets your attention. There were about a million places I would have rather been besides that room. Still, I didn't flinch.

Of course, the therapy didn't work for me, but I have no doubt I tolerated it so well, in part, because of my attitude. This type of situation presented itself hundreds of times over the years. Whether it was chemo or a blood transfusion, I just assumed the treatment would work as advertised and improve my situation. To a large degree, it became a self-fulfilling prophecy.

Of course, everyone knows this as the placebo effect. There is also the nocebo effect, where people feel ill, just because they believe they will feel ill. Dr. Elaine Fox, in her book "Rainy Brain, Sunny Brain," tells the story of a man who was diagnosed with terminal liver cancer. He was given a few months to live, and as expected, he passed away in the estimated time period. His doctors were shocked when a post-mortem revealed no cancer was present. The patient had simply heard a diagnosis and his body followed as his mind directed.

I didn't know it at the time, but the way I approached my chemo was a perfect example of how everyday stress and anxiety do not come from external events, but from our interpretation of those events. This leads to the same diagnosis or chemo being understood and processed in varied and diverse ways by different patients. It's what goes on between our ears that really matters in how we perceive and ultimately deal with our illness.

What I experienced as I dealt with my disease can be explained by the research studies performed in the field known as psychoneuroimmunology. This is where the links between the psychological process and the immune system are explored. Immune cells respond to signals from the central nervous system. And in return, immune cells produce cytokines (protein molecules that work in cellular communication) that act on the central nervous system.

As a result of this kind of interaction, we tend to get what we expect. It happens every day to all of us. Literature is teeming with examples. If given decaf coffee by mistake, people will still get that wired feeling. And according to University of Washington research, people given non-alcoholic beer, when they believed they were consuming regular beer, acted drunk just the same.

In one of my favorite stories, several people fell ill at a football stadium. Management immediately shut down a drink station that was suspected of being the cause. An announcement was made over the PA that if anyone had purchased a drink from that station and was feeling ill, they could report to the first aid booth. In minutes, a long line had formed with several nauseous individuals throwing up.

Meanwhile, stadium management determined there was nothing wrong with the drink station and made an announcement over the PA to that effect. Several minutes later, the majority of the fans had left their place in the first aid line and returned to their seats. Clearly, there is a very strong connection between our thoughts and our bodies.

One of my friends (a doctor) gave me a great piece of advice. He suggested that I focus my thoughts during meditation on the body I had pre-illness. Just like someone might dream of a tropical beach to help relax, I would do well to dream of running my favorite trail. If we train the mind to remember its former healthy state, the body will follow.

Though I was living with aplastic anemia, I was determined not to be defined by it. To the greatest extent possible, I would still be the same person I was pre-illness. I didn't realize it at the time, but that attitude was a life saver. A 2012 article by Erik Angner in the Journal of Happiness Studies (yes, there really is a journal with that name) found that happiness is not directly impacted by disease, but more by the extent to which the disease affects and disrupts daily life. For example, cancer was found to have a smaller influence on happiness, than other less threatening conditions, such as urinary continence which is a major disruption to daily life.

The article noted that most newly diagnosed patients start adapting immediately to their new limitations. Those who adapt the best and find contentment in other parts of their lives usually are the happiest. I was used to finding enjoyment in hiking and running, and I needed to find other activities that I would enjoy. For the most part, I was content with walking, gardening, and yoga. The adjustments I had to make were substantial and against my will, but I was determined to accept them. I would not allow them to change who I was in mind or body. When illness strikes, roll with the changes, keep a great attitude, and stay true to who you are.

How attitude affects our body is an area of much research. Dr. Elaine Fox writes: "Optimism is not so much about feeling happy, nor necessarily a belief that everything will be fine, but about how we respond when times get tough. Optimists tend to keep going, even when it seems as if the whole world is against them."

She offers practical advice, saying that the key difference in optimists is not that they just have a positive attitude, but that they take action. Having a sense of control over your situation and your life is essential. This way when you suffer a setback, such as disease or illness, you will be equipped to do something about it.

Clinicians have told me that for most patients' disposition and outlook does not change because of an illness. You will be the same person, seeing the glass half full or half empty, unless you go out and actively make changes.

My hematologist, Dr. Burt Alexander, constantly sees the strong link between attitude and outcome in his patients. He's observed many patients who weren't expected to live more than a few weeks, but far exceeded their prognosis and lived for many months. Their common trait was they all carried a good attitude. The reverse is also true. He remembers a lady who wasn't gravely ill and should have lived for months, but upon hearing Dr. Alexander's diagnosis, she quietly told him, "I'm ready to go." She passed in 48 hours.

When Dr. Alexander encounters a patient with a bad attitude, he urges them to change it. He encourages people to read books, listen to tapes, investigate a life coach, but most importantly, surround yourself with positive people. The power of positive people is contagious and should not be underestimated. Much in the same way we can change our diet or exercise habits, we can change our attitude.

It is thought that a tendency towards positive thinking is influenced by genes that control the neurotransmitters in the brain. I believe I am one of the lucky ones, blessed with that inclination. However, we can all change our environment, work on how we interpret everyday stress, and retrain our brains to think with a happy bias. And that should give everyone hope, that with some work, many characteristics of positive thinking can be learned, even as adults.

ERIC HODIES

# CHAPTER 5 ~ GET MOVING

*"Those who think they have not time for bodily exercise will sooner or later have to find time for illness"*
*- Edward Stanley, Earl of Derby,1873*

For ten years, I played a little game. Every time I left the house and went for a walk, I made believe each step would take me one step closer to health. I didn't care if my cure was millions of steps in the distance; I would inch a little closer to it each day. I'm nothing, if not persistent. Given enough time, I could get there or anywhere. So each day, I stepped out the front door, put one foot in front of the other, and pursued my imaginary target.

Sometimes I walked a little and sometimes a lot. But I always returned just a little bit better for it and a tiny, but not insignificant amount closer to my goal.

It was a silly game, but it worked on several different levels. My body (particularly my immune system) thrived on the activity and it gave me a daily jolt of well-being and a sense of accomplishment. Most importantly, it was something practical that I could do each and every day to help myself. After ten years of walking and over 20 million steps, I regained my health.

Of course, all that walking did not lead directly to my cure. And everyone, including myself, was shocked by my remission. But there was an undeniable connection between those millions of steps and regaining my health. How could there not be? Our bodies are meant for moving.

There are proven physiological processes that occur as we exercise that keep us young and ward off disease. Exercise is systemic, and these effects occur in almost every cell of your body. Staying active is the fountain of youth and a vaccine against many future health problems, all rolled into one.

If a doctor could write a prescription for exercise, it would probably allow you to eliminate most of your other medications. Exercise imparts vitality, confidence, and stamina, without any side effects. It boosts the immune system, promotes sleep, stimulates bone growth, and improves circulation. It can also help prevent or manage many health concerns, including diabetes and weight control.

In addition, the endorphins released during exercise resemble opiates and have a similar mood altering effect. This results in an improved mood and sense of well-being. Fitness author Bill Phillips has said, "Food is the most widely abused anti-anxiety drug in America, and exercise is the most potent yet underutilized anti-depressant."

Exercise also has immediate benefits for each and every cell in your body. As you go through normal daily living, the cells in your body collect leftover pieces of broken and worn out intracellular components. Basically, a junkyard of waste forms inside your cells.

Cells have ways to eliminate or recycle this junk. However, it's believed that when this process stops working efficiently and waste products build up, diseases tend to develop. Exercise can counteract this and increase the rate of waste product removal. If you are sick and your body is under great stress, it is imperative to do your daily bit to keep your body in motion.

People tend to stop being active after they receive a diagnosis. Only a handful of times in hundreds of conversations with fellow patients did I get an affirmative response when I asked if they were exercising. A common response was that since they've been struck with an awful diagnosis, it can't do any good to exercise now. They wanted to conserve energy thinking they will be aiding their body during treatment. Both statements could not be further from the truth.

In the past, people with disease related fatigue were advised to rest. However, the tide has changed. A 2012 Cochrane Collaboration review of 4068 cancer patients with solid tumors, primarily breast and prostate cancers, found that exercise decreased, not increased, cancer-related fatigue. Interestingly, it showed that aerobic exercise, such walking and cycling, had a significant effect, but resistance training did not.

When you're dealing with a chronic disease, everything seems so overwhelming. Exercise just doesn't seem like a high priority when you have prescriptions to go fill, insurance issues to tackle, and doctor appointments to travel to, not to mention the rest of life that continues on in spite of our health issues. However, this is when exercise is most important.

Start by doing away with the notion that exercise is only for the fit or to get fit. This isn't about getting in shape to compete. It's not even about playing a sport or the way you look. This is about your health. Any and all kinds of activity are worthwhile and will benefit your health.

Everyone should be encouraged to do some kind of

activity, whatever is appropriate for their energy levels. There may be days when you can do very little. The focus should be on what you can do, and not on what you can't do or used to be able to do. Previous athletic achievements count for nothing. The exercise you do when you are fighting an illness has a far more important goal: Keeping you healthy, so you can get well again.

Of course, any exercise program should be discussed with your doctor. The human body has warning signs to let us know if we are going beyond where we should. Learn to discern the difference between being tired and being exhausted. Listen to your body, it will tell you how it's feeling.

To get the desired effect from exercise, it's not necessary to hit the gym for hours or run for miles. You just have to put your body into motion. Biking, walking, and yoga are great. Housework and gardening will work, too. A safe and effective alternative to moderate intensity conventional exercise is Tai Chi. It is often referred to as "Meditation in Motion" but some are now calling it "Medication in Motion" because of its calming influence. Practicing Tai Chi has been linked to many positive effects, such as lower stress, better balance, and improved blood flow. Carol and I have been taking lessons and are enjoying it.

If you are in the hospital and can only walk a few

rooms in one direction and then back, there is benefit in that, too. And for some, just getting out of bed is an accomplishment. If you can, exercising outdoors is usually more invigorating than doing it indoors. Whatever you decide to do, make sure it's fun and you enjoy it.

Recent research shows that it takes even less activity to get health benefits than previously thought. Noted wellness and fitness author, Gretchen Reynolds, says most of the prolonged life benefits and reduced disease risks come in the first 20 minutes of activity. If you exercise for more than that, then it is primarily for fitness. Science shows that even standing for 20 minutes produces positive physiological changes.

Moving your body takes work. It will elevate your heart rate, increase your breathing and fatigue your muscles. You will want to stop. It will make you tired, or even exhausted, in the short term. Your head may try to talk your body into stopping. Always keep in mind why you are doing it.

With dedication and persistence, it will gradually get easier. But even as you improve, there will be days when motivation is elusive. Even Olympic athletes have bad days. This is a journey with ups and downs, but keeping it fun will help you stay on track. And when it gets easier, that's your cue to find new goals and challenge yourself to do more.

Just as activity is beneficial, inactivity carries its own health risks. This is particularly important if you are ill. There is a scientific discipline devoted to inactivity physiology and the changes that the body undergoes at rest. The research being conducted is shedding light on the positive physiological changes that occur during activity and negative changes that occur during rest.

During prolonged stretches of inactivity, such as watching television or working on a computer, the large muscles of the body do not contract. In this state, these muscles don't require fuel, causing blood sugar to accumulate and contributing to diabetes and other illnesses. Obviously, spending nearly every minute of a day in a hospital bed is detrimental to anyone. I wonder how many patients would have better outcomes if encouraged to walk a little each day.

Of significance is that the changes made during exercise do not undo the changes that occur during inactivity. So, just as essential as it is to exercise at least 20 minutes daily, it is equally important to resist inactivity for hours on end. Accordingly, even if you exercise, get up from your computer or couch every hour. A great idea is to always stand when talking on the phone.

Naturally, being overweight carries all sorts of health risks, including cardiovascular disease, diabetes, and certain types of cancer. Next to not smoking, losing weight is the single most important thing you can do to get healthy. However, even if you are overweight and don't lose an ounce of fat, the benefits of being active are still real.

Don't put off being active until you've been diagnosed with an illness. You will need all the weapons you can muster in your fight. Exercise now and make your body stronger. If your health isn't up to par, you will be at a disadvantage if you must endure a long period of illness.

I lived with aplastic anemia for nine years before my remission. In that time, I subjected my body to chemo treatments and transfusions, and ingested enough medications to sink a ship. I'm convinced that my previous health and fitness level was vital in tolerating the rigors of an illness of such long duration. When I was diagnosed, I had no other medical issues to complicate my treatment. I did not have high blood pressure, diabetes, heart disease or any other chronic ailment. I wasn't taking a single medication. My body took a pretty good beating living with my disease, but I endured it, in part, because of the benefits derived from years of exercise.

On my way to the ultimate goal of getting healthy, I enjoyed small victories on most days I went for a walk. I felt a sense of accomplishment. Stress dissipated. Walking was a distraction from medical related thoughts, and my mind wandered as I put one foot in front of the other. Spending time outdoors with nature was invigorating, and the sun was my drug. There was hardly a day that I did not finish feeling more refreshed and energized than when I walked out the door. Most importantly, I returned home with an awareness that my body was still quite strong and capable of withstanding whatever would be thrown at it next.

We are designed to move and it comes naturally. Inactivity is unnatural. Get moving.

ERIC HODIES

# CHAPTER 6 ~ EAT RIGHT

*"If you don't take care of your body, where else are you going to live?"*

*- Trevor Romain, author*

I've been conscious of good nutrition for as long as I can remember. I even became a vegetarian my senior year in high school. I wish I could say I did it for animal rights, but back then I was more interested in my running performance. It was an article in Runner's World magazine that put the idea in my head. Although I wasn't as fast as I would have liked (who is?), I was competitive, and I thought being a vegetarian would help me run faster.

At the time, I also considered taking bee pollen, as that was being touted as the latest and greatest performance enhancer. I stuck to my vegetarian ways, but passed on taking the bee pollen. Though tempting, I couldn't buy into the belief that a single food item could make me run faster. I decided to hold onto the hard earned cash I made from a paper route I shared with a friend. To skip the bee pollen just seemed intuitive at the time, but in hindsight, this would be the birth of my "Eat the Damn Carrot" philosophy of eating.

I was a bit of an outcast around the dinner table, as this was well before veggie burgers and other meatless products hit grocery stores. In spite of that, I stayed with it. I didn't notice an improvement in my running performance, so after five years, I went back to being an omnivore. Following my vegetarian days, I continued my healthy lifestyle and stayed current on nutrition. However, it wasn't until I received my diagnosis that I realized how my life literally depends on the foods I put into my body. Just because my running times didn't improve as a vegetarian, it didn't mean that my diet hadn't made me healthier on the inside, where it counts the most.

We all have trillions of cells that require constant and never ending maintenance and replacement. The cells lining our stomach last only five days. The entire surface layer of the skin is replaced every two weeks. And even the entire human skeleton is replaced every 10 years. All that fixing, repairing, and maintenance can only happen by providing our bodies with all the necessary building materials. And that can only happen by eating right.

Upon diagnosis, it became my goal to feed the cells in my body every nutrient necessary in order for them to work at peak efficiency. This would help keep my body as strong as possible to withstand the chemotherapies that would hurt and weaken my body. Though I didn't realize it at the time, it would also aid me in staying alive for a spontaneous remission that would not occur until nine years after my diagnosis.

This "eat right" mentality is at the heart of my "Eat the Damn Carrot" philosophy. Getting back to the basics and eating nutritious food is a positive step that everyone can take and its benefits start immediately. Whether you are healthy or sick, young or old, what you put into your body will make a difference in your health.

Start right now by putting only healthy foods on your plate. A doctor can prescribe you an antibiotic which will only treat a single illness, the bacteria that is currently making your body sick. But your food choices have the power to prevent and even reverse many serious chronic illnesses. Health educator Ann Wigmore says, "The food you eat can either be the safest and most powerful form of medicine or the slowest form of poison." Let's discuss the foods that we should eat and the ones we should avoid.

## What to Eat

Of course, aplastic anemia is not a disease based on a nutritional deficiency, so I knew my cure wasn't simply a matter of eating some amazing supplement or super food, gulping mega doses of vitamins, or brewing an exotic herb with a strange sounding name grown in a remote part of Asia.

It is very common when an individual is faced with a devastating diagnosis that they make radical changes in their diet. Usually there is a search for the elusive miracle cure, supplement, and/or drug. I wanted that miracle cure as much as the next person, but I knew that existed only in dreams. Instead I took a common sense approach to eating. I ate with the goal of nourishing my body to the maximum and maintaining as healthy a body as possible, not with the expectation of a miracle cure. My aim has always been to enjoy the process and to keep it fun.

Eating well is simple. Noted food author Michael Pollan boils it down into seven words, "Eat food. Not too much. Mostly plants." Those first two words may sound obvious, but it's not until you recognize that many of the items on the grocery store shelves are more like "food products" than actual food, before you can be on your way to a healthier diet.

The foods I put on my plate are based on a whole

foods plant based diet. Simply put, if it comes from a plant, then it's ok to eat. That includes whole or minimally processed vegetables, fruits, nuts, legumes, and whole grains. If it's a whole food, there should be only one ingredient, like beans or barley. If these foods are minimally processed, they will look similar to the way they were grown. For instance, a pop tart does not look like any food I've ever seen growing in a field. Michael Pollan advises to not eat anything your grandparents wouldn't recognize.

There really are very few rules on a simple whole foods plant based diet. The entire produce section is fair game. In that area, you won't have to worry about the obvious red flags. No heavy processing or artificial anything found there. And if you want to know what not to eat, go visit any gas station or drive through window.

Eating well is not complicated, but we tend to make it complicated. We spend billions of dollars on nutritionists, vitamins, supplements, books, and computer programs, all in the goal of helping us eat right. Each week there seems to be another new diet, vitamin, or supplement that promises to make us smarter or lead to ultimate health and vitality. It's easy to get confused. In reality, there are no shortcuts and no super diets, only simple nutritious foods.

Eating this way, meats, saturated fats, and simple carbohydrates (sugar, breads and pastas) should be a very minor part of the diet, if at all. By focusing on a wide variety of plant based foods, it's not necessary to count every calorie, nutrient, or gram of fiber. I never worry if I'm getting all that is necessary. The foods I put on my plate supply everything I need. (Horses and elephants eat strict plant based diets and their large muscles don't lack for protein.) Besides, making food choices based on vitamin, mineral, or fiber content usually isn't wise.

Many cereals and frozen pizzas are fortified with vitamins, but most of those selections will not deliver good nutrition. There are simply too many dubious man made ingredients in those highly processed products and not enough of the good stuff. My aim is to free my body of that artificial junk and instead feed my hungry cells with the phytochemicals, antioxidants, and micronutrients that can be found in abundance in a plant based diet.

Though the health benefits of eating a vegetarian diet are significant, my aim isn't to turn every reader into a vegetarian. That wouldn't be a reasonable expectation, but it should be a realistic goal to reduce the amount of meat we eat. Diets high in animal fat are associated with greater risks of several cancers. In addition, heart disease, the number one killer in America, is at least partially caused by the build-up of cholesterol and saturated fat from animal meat. More reasons to reduce meat intake will be discussed under

"What not to Eat."

A complete nutritious diet can't be duplicated through pills and supplements.

Researchers and chemists have been trying for years to isolate vitamins, minerals, antioxidants and phytochemicals in order to put them in a pill for easy, convenient consumption. However, food chemistry is complex, and we simply can't extract one vitamin or mineral and expect it to be effective without the support of everything that occurs naturally.

Something that is man-made will never be superior to eating foods in their natural state. For example, a recent study found that vegetarians are 30 to 40 percent less likely to develop cataracts compared to meat eaters. However, in 2011, a significant study, conducted at Harvard over an eight year period, found that vitamin C and E supplements did not reduce the risk of cataracts. It is increasingly evident that taking these antioxidants in supplement form does not have the same effect as eating them as nature intended.

Nature does it so well that researchers often refer to the combinations and optimal range of potency found in whole foods as the "Goldilocks phenomenon." For instance, too little vitamin C can result in scurvy, while too much Vitamin C can increase the risk of kidney stones. Eat some fruit and get just the right amount. Another example is the Caret (Carotene and Retinol Efficacy Trial) study that was stopped early when it was found that high doses of Vitamin A and E, which were hoped to decrease lung cancer, were instead found to increase the risks of lung cancer.

Clearly, our mothers were right and we should eat all our vegetables. The goal should be that each meal includes several servings of different colored vegetables. If everyone reverted back to the basics and began eating the unprocessed foods that the earth provides, we would hardly have a need for vitamin and mineral manufacturers.

If eating lots of different vegetables sounds boring and monotonous, I must say I don't eat like a bird or live like a monk (pick your metaphor), and I'm not proposing you do either. Although some people may find the meals served in our house to be a little top heavy in the vegetables and beans department, I never feel like I am missing out on anything. Quite the contrary, I feel empowered by all the nutritious foods I put on my plate and in my body.

We always keep our fridge full of fruits and vegetables. You can shop at a health food store if you like, but everything you need is in the produce department of a well-stocked grocery store. You can also spend six bucks for a carrot and wheat germ smoothie at the same health food store, but that will buy you a larger variety of fresh vegetables at your grocery store that can be worked into several meals.

You can prepare your vegetables a number of different ways. I steam my veggies, put them in soups (lentil soup is a favorite), stir fry them, or use as a filling in whole grain wraps. Our cupboard has containers of spelt, quinoa, barley and other whole grains. My pasta is always whole grain unless I am at a restaurant. Then there are substitutions, like portobello mushrooms on a whole grain bun instead of a hamburger. There are always new foods to explore and new recipes to try. I don't look at it as a diet or something to dread, but as a way of living.

I enjoy knowing exactly what I'm putting in my body. I make my own granola, changing up the recipe often, but usually including rolled oats, diced apples, almond slivers, and cinnamon. On most Sundays, I bake a pan of breakfast bars that last all week. I don't work from a recipe, but instead throw all kinds of seeds, nuts, and fruits into these bars. I use whole grain flours and substitute applesauce for oil. Almost any ingredient in the house is fair game until the pan is heavy and fully loaded. These bars practically ooze health and they have taken on a life of their own. A friend of mine from work, in a nod to the number of ingredients and their brick-like appearance, affectionately refers to the bars as trash loaf.

Instead of routine and boring salads, we try to keep it interesting by adding different vegetables, such as artichoke hearts, avocado slices, walnuts and berries. We also substitute sunflower or pumpkin seeds for the croutons. Breakfast is an ideal time to load up on antioxidants. Try adding berries, nuts, seeds, flax seed and Greek yogurt to a whole grain cereal. We occasionally use our juicer, but more often we make smoothies using almond milk, Greek yogurt, bananas, and mixed berries. As long as it is real food, feel free to use whatever ingredients suit your taste.

There are plenty of strict diets out there, like a raw foods diet, but my diet provides me the best nutrition without compromising my lifestyle. I don't want to live my life in absolutes with foods, including meat, that can't ever be touched. Life is too short. Some people would label me a semi-vegetarian, and others would say I'm not a vegetarian at all. That doesn't matter. It's important to make compromises, and to that end, I strive to make healthy choices about 80 percent of the time. That leaves at least a couple of meals a week that allow me to "cheat" or indulge a little.

For starters, I enjoy a once a week serving of wild caught salmon, and the associated omega-3 fatty acids have been linked to greater heart and brain health. I also live in the real world with friends, restaurants, holidays, and cook-outs all a part of my life. At restaurants, I can usually order items like a bean burrito or a pizza without meat toppings. Instead of detracting from my health, an occasional restaurant meal can add variety and provide a break from the usual meals. One of life's pleasures is a homemade just out-of-the-oven chocolate chip cookie, and you will never find me passing on one of those.

The two fun meals a week is also a great time to try some new foods. If you eat healthy the majority of the time, you won't feel guilty or have to scramble for excuses when the family wants to grill out or friends want to meet for dinner. Just like one nutritious meal won't make you healthy, one bad meal won't make you unhealthy.

Sometimes the hard part is just taking the first step. For some, it can be difficult to change decades of bad habits. And it may seem like eating an abundance of vegetables isn't making a difference. You have to be able to enjoy the process, not just the end result. Don't eat avocadoes when you detest them, just because some expert in a magazine or on a television show says you should eat them. That won't do anything, except make you hate what you're doing. There are plenty of other fruits and vegetables out there.

Sure, the payoff is better health, but the practice of trying new vegetables and new recipes should also be part of the fun. By getting caught up in the excitement of the process, your mindset will slowly change, and soon you will believe that you are transforming your life, one meal at a time.

Another way to make it easier is to incorporate your family and friends into your new found love for clean eating. Surround yourself with like-minded folks, try new recipes with friends, and make the trip to a farmers market a family outing.

I eat the way I do because I enjoy it and I believe in it. When I was at my lowest point and my disease was getting the best of me, putting the best foods possible on my plate gave me something very practical to do. I felt like I was helping to cure myself, when nothing else had helped. I was giving my body, which had never let me down before, a fighting chance.

For some, these are big steps, and for others they may even seem extreme. I completely understand. If you've never been diagnosed with a chronic disease, you won't feel that urgency to rethink your food choices. But if your health is under attack and your life is being threatened, you need to dig deep, evaluate your food choices, and feed your body only the good stuff. Even the smallest nutritional changes in your diet will make a difference. I know it did with me.

## What not to Eat

Avoid any foods containing trans fats, saturated fats, high fructose corn syrup, artificial sweeteners, dyes, antibiotics, hormones, added sugars, added sodium, genetically modified foods (GMOs), and preservatives. Whew, that's a long list. But it's not as daunting as it appears. If you put your effort into eating the foods that are healthy, you will end up eating little, if anything, unhealthy.

By far, the single most important action you can take is to read the ingredient list of everything you purchase. As a result of intensive food processing, we ingest a spectrum of additives, dyes, hormones, and preservatives with unknown long term effects on humans. Thanks to ingredient lists, you have the power to know what foods contain these additives and to take control of what you put in your body. Make it a habit and you will be on your way to healthier eating and a healthier body.

If you consistently read ingredient lists and choose foods with short lists, you will automatically eliminate many unhealthy additives. If you see foods containing dyes, preservatives, or artificial sweeteners put it back on the shelf. The same with trans fats and high fructose corn syrup. If the ingredient list contains sodium nitrite or BHA, leave it on the shelf. If a food has sugar listed as one of the first few ingredients, walk right past it. And if there is something listed that you don't recognize as a food, don't buy it.

Those ingredient lists can be a real wake-up call. As a

general rule, the more a food is processed, the more likely it will contain unhealthy ingredients. Many items on grocery store shelves and in the frozen foods aisle are really more like food products than real foods. As you read ingredient lists, you will come across heavily processed foods that come in boxes or packages routinely list more than 20 ingredients. Conversely, when you choose fresh produce, no food label is required because nothing is added to them.

Trans fat, sodium, and sugar are the heavy hitters with the greatest negative impact on health. Trans fats increase the shelf life of many baked goods, but will reduce your own shelf life. There is overwhelming evidence that diets higher in trans fats significantly raise the risk of having a stroke and heart attack. You can identify trans fats by looking for the words "partially hydrogenated."

Nearly every American consumes too much sodium, thereby raising blood pressure, which can lead to reduced kidney function and kidney damage. My kidneys were already working overtime, as a number of my medications were eliminated through the kidneys. The thought of making my kidneys work any harder than they already were was motivation enough to reduce my sodium. Avoid products with sodium in the name, such as monosodium glutamate, sodium citrate, or disodium phosphate. As an alternative, use herbs for seasoning, and get more antioxidants as a bonus.

Sugar has such a far reaching negative impact on health, that some equate the dangers of sugar to the dangers of alcohol and tobacco. Sugar is a major contributor to obesity, diabetes, heart disease, and cancer, but what got my attention was sugar's ability to cause an inflammatory response and reduction in the immune system. Just the sugar from a soda is enough to noticeably reduce the ability of white cells to fight bacteria. If you are ill, stay away from sugar and give your immune system a fighting chance.

A few seconds spent reading food labels is well worth it. I walked the cereal aisle and found several cereals with five or fewer ingredients sitting alongside several cereals with ingredient lists in excess of 30 items. And that's not counting the added vitamins and minerals. Many of those 30 ingredients are substances that are foreign to me and sound like they belong in a chemistry set. Not surprisingly, these cereals list more than a half dozen sources of sugar. In spite of all that, every one of these cereals had some form of marketing on the front of the box touting the nutritional benefit of the cereal.

The buzz words printed on food packaging can be very misleading. Just because a food is touted to be multi-grain, natural, omega 3 fortified or even organic doesn't mean it's not heavily processed. A product that touts itself as multigrain is likely just several refined grains. You want to look for the words "whole grain." Many foods that are marked as "natural" are far from it. The FDA doesn't have a definition that foods must comply with in order carry that label. Are organic cookies healthy? Not unless it's important that your sugar and white flour come from organic sources. It's still a heavily processed, nutritionally empty food, which is a nice way of saying junk food.

It seems like most healthy foods have a heavily processed evil twin sitting right next to it on the food shelf. Oatmeal is healthy, right? It is if you buy the package that lists one ingredient, oats. If you buy the processed flavored instant kind, especially the one that comes in the packets, be prepared to ingest all kinds of added sugar and preservatives.

Even foods widely accepted as healthy may have excessive ingredient lists. A very popular brand of veggie burgers has over 30 ingredients listed on the package. Only a very few of those ingredients are soy and vegetables, the bulk are man-made additives (with questionable long term effects) that help with the taste and shelf life of the product. Granted some are vitamins, but even those I would prefer to get in the form and ratios that nature intended.

I've met people who skip their medications or simply won't take an aspirin because of fear of introducing something unnatural into their body. But these same people will eat food products containing dozens of hard to pronounce man-made ingredients of dubious nature, many sounding like they belong in a chemistry class lecture. What's the difference?

These man-made additives, dyes and preservatives have been linked to health problems, and are under great debate as to their long term health risks. Eliminate any risk by cutting out anything questionable and choosing most of your foods from the produce aisle, not the frozen foods aisle (with the exception of frozen vegetables). And if the foods you are buying are packed in cans or boxes, try to limit the number of ingredients to five or fewer. Make it a habit to read food labels.

Meat intake has been strongly linked to cardiovascular disease and some cancers, but the health risks of eating meat is also a result of the manner in which the animal was raised. Food production is big business, so there is always constant pressure to grow or raise the largest quantity of food for the least amount of money. Quality of food is secondary, and farmers turn to heavy use of antibiotics and growth hormones to help them. An amazing 80% of the antibiotics produced in this country are fed to livestock. The result of eating that meat is we make ourselves more susceptible to bacteria. With some strains of bacteria becoming antibiotic resistant, why would you want to increase your risk of infection even slightly?

Then there are the growth hormones given to livestock. The six weeks of a chicken's miserable life is spent in crowded buildings with little ventilation and no room to move. If you ever watch a video of how the large producers raise chickens, it is not something you will soon forget. Thus far my reasons to go meatless have been for the sake of health, but this is the point where the inhumane treatment of these animals influences my eating habits.

When you see how the chickens are raised, it won't surprise you that the Humane Society asserts that 90% of chickens have detectable leg problems and structural deformities. These growth hormones a chicken is fed enable it to grow at a phenomenal rate. The University of Arkansas reports that if a man grew at the same rate as a chicken, he would weigh 349 pounds by his second birthday.

A study, released in 2012 from the Johns Hopkins University Center for a Livable Future, sheds light on the extent that additives are added to livestock. They tested poultry and found the expected additives and hormones, plus surprises such as caffeine, active ingredients of Tylenol and Benadryl, banned antibiotics, and arsenic. All these substances have the sole purpose of keeping meat production up by keeping livestock healthy.

The high saturated fat content of meat is a risk factor in heart health and cancer. Loma Linda has completed a series of studies on members of the Seventh Day Adventist Church (largely vegetarians). They found the vegetarians had lower rates of most cancers, including cancers of the stomach, colon, rectum, and prostate. It is believed that this is likely due to less exposure to the carcinogens and mutagens found in meat. Many studies have also demonstrated links between those people with a high dietary intake of fruits and vegetables (specifically foods high in antioxidants) and a reduced risk of many diseases.

Processed meats, such as hot dogs and bacon, are especially risky because of the nitrites that appear to promote cancers. Exactly what the health risks are to consuming any meat that has been treated with growth hormones, additives, and antibiotics is still being debated and probably will be for some time. But it makes good sense to avoid it. If you do eat meat, at least eliminate the processed meats, reduce your intake of other meats, and buy organic.

I struggle to limit my dairy intake. Like many, I love cheese, and vegetarian substitutes just don't taste like the real thing. The debate continues as to the health risks, if any, of dairy products. Meanwhile, we're the only species to drink another species' milk, as cow milk is designed to meet the needs of a calf to grow into a large cow, not for human nutrition. Thus, the protein, fat, and sugar (lactose) content are different than that of human milk. Not surprisingly, a milk allergy is one of the most common allergies, and many people don't realize it until they eliminate it from their diet. With all the different flavored almond, rice and soy milks available, it's hard not to find something enjoyable to pour on your cereal.

It's easy to eat well on a plant based diet. However, there are a few pitfalls, even with apparently healthy foods. Pasta is a good example. Whole grain pasta can be a great source of fiber and energy, but often times it is loaded with fat and sodium, as a result of the sauces added to it. In addition, unless you select organic brands, most grains are genetically modified (GMO). Baked potatoes are another example of a good food often ruined by the toppings added to it.

Soy products are another case where the plant (soy bean) starts out nutritious, but processing often introduces questionable changes to the food. Even the innocent and ubiquitous veggie burger is a victim of this processing. In order to change the soy protein into a veggie burger, manufacturers process it with hexane. Eat at your own risk, as hexane is classified as an air pollutant by the EPA and a neurotoxin by the CDC. Although it is unknown how much hexane is still in the food after the processing and if it presents a health risk, it seems only sensible to avoid it. Only choose organic brands, as hexane is banned in foods produced organically.

In addition to the hexane residue, most veggie

burgers also contain oils heavy in omega 6 fatty acids and ingredients that have been genetically modified. I've stopped eating manufactured veggie burgers to avoid anything questionable, and make my own. I've found many great recipes online, and most require only 20 minutes or so of prep work. My patties are made with a few simple whole foods, like lentils, chick peas, sweet potatoes, olive oil, and spices. It's so much more empowering to eat the real food as nature intended instead of a manufactured product concocted in a factory. In other words, eat the damn carrot.

At best, soft drinks are junk, and at worst they are detrimental to your health. Most contain high fructose corn syrup, phosphoric acid, citric acid, and a host of other chemicals. Diet drinks also have artificial sweeteners, and the word artificial should be enough of a tip off to avoid them. The high fructose corn syrup results in insulin spikes and has been linked to obesity, cardiovascular disease, and diabetes. (Graphs of per capita consumption of high fructose corn syrup versus incidence of diabetes indicate a very strong correlation.) The phosphoric acid leaches calcium out of your bones, contributing to osteoporosis. And the acidity of the drink can lead to the risk of tooth damage through dental erosion. I don't want a "food" like that in my body.

My purpose isn't to take away all the fun in eating, but

to bring awareness to what you are eating. It's easy to assume any food that makes its way to a grocery store shelf is innocuous, but that isn't the case. Much of what is added to our food has not been studied for long term safety. There is pressure to make the government require additional information on labeling, but the food industry is resisting. Recently, much attention has been focused on the lack of regulations for the labeling of genetically modified organisms.

In 2012, the FDA gave preliminary approval to allow the farming of genetically modified salmon, dubbed "frankenfish" by some, despite the lack of any independent long term studies. This fish could be for sale in your grocery store soon and without labels identifying its origins. For now, I will pass on any genetically engineered food, thank-you very much. I encourage you to think about where your food came from, the manner in which it was processed, what exactly was added to it, and if you want it in your body.

If you want to eat healthy, you simply must eat at home as much as possible. Very few restaurants offer truly healthy selections. Most are loaded with sodium, butter, and oils, and frequently at extra-large portion sizes. A study for the journal Public Health Nutrition looked at 30,923 menu items from 245 brands of restaurants. It found 96 percent of those meals failed recommendations regarding intake of calories, sodium, fat, and saturated fat as set by the U.S. Department of Agriculture. For instance, the Cheesecake Factory's Bistro Shrimp Pasta has 89 grams of saturated fat. Assuming that on an average day I consume 5-8 grams of saturated fat, mostly from nuts and cheese, that single plate of pasta represents two weeks of saturated fat for me.

Even restaurants touting healthy meals usually serve dishes made with plenty of oil, butter and salt. Fast food, in particular, is specifically designed to taste good by means of secret formulas of additives. As reported in Time magazine, a McDonald's McRib sandwich contains an astounding 70 ingredients, including azodicarbonamide, a flour bleaching agent often used in the production of foamed plastics. Yet, I've eaten at several hospital cafeterias featuring kiosks of well-known fast food chains.

Finally, to visually see the link between diet and disease, look at the following graph of Type 2 diabetes as a function of obesity. The risk of Type 2 diabetes is heavily influenced by weight and food choices.

## 'Relationship between BMI and Type 2 Diabetes'

*Source:* http://www.cutthewaist.com/impact.html

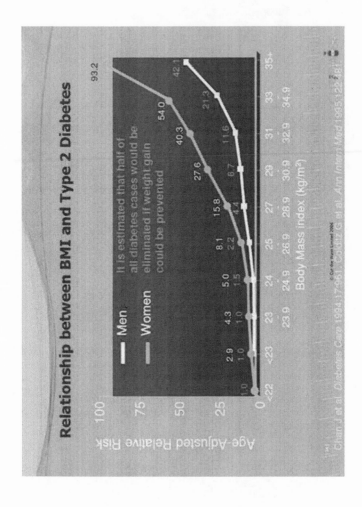

It seems counterintuitive to spend billions of dollars on new medicines to treat diabetes and many other chronic illnesses when we can focus our efforts on the root of the problem - our diet.

Just eat the damn carrot.

## Nutrition for hospitals and doctors

I had hundreds of medical appointments over a 10 year span, and not once was I ever asked about my nutrition. Not a single time. There were days, as a chemo patient in the hospital, when I was barely eating and my body was in a weakened state. Still, nutrition was just not part of my medical treatment, in any way, shape, or form. I was also never asked if I wanted to speak to a dietitian. I'm sure I could have seen a dietitian if I had only asked, but the point is that nutrition is not at the forefront of medical care.

In hospitals, there are certain diagnoses or criteria that will automatically trigger a nutrition consult from a dietitian. This leaves many people who don't trigger a consult, but would certainly benefit from a dietitian's input. In order for these patients to receive a nutrition consult, their doctor would have to order the consult or the patient would have to request a visit by a dietitian.

Unfortunately, many patients do not know to ask to

see a dietitian, and many doctors do not recognize the overall importance of nutrition to disease and healing. In medical school, doctors are taught about disease, care management and medications and are only required to take one nutrition class. They certainly cannot be the experts in everything; therefore, a multidisciplinary approach is required for the overall well-being of each and every patient.

I also found that hospitals differed greatly on their approach to nutrition. Some hospitals have great programs, such as the one where there was a dedicated kitchen serving the bone marrow transplant floor. Others hospitals were not as careful, such as the one that served me lettuce while my immune system had been decimated by chemo. Bone marrow transplant patients and immune compromised patients should avoid eating raw fruit and vegetables because of the risk of germs from improperly washed produce. Ironically, the same hospital that served me lettuce would only allow me to drink bottled water.

Clearly, it's hard enough selecting a hospital based on treatment choices, much less their nutritional program. For the most part, I took matters into my own hands by bringing my own food in each day. My request to have my lunch warmed up was never refused, though I tried to time it for when the staff wasn't so busy. I knew what was in my food, how it was prepared, and who handled it. I rarely ate hospital food. Not coincidently, I never picked up a stomach bug or had any kind of intestinal distress.

But awareness is growing and there is a shift in attitude. New York City, known for its crackdown on supersize sugar drinks, is now changing the way food is served in the city's hospitals. Though the Healthy Hospital Food Initiative is voluntary, it covers many aspects of hospital food, from banning of deep fryers to making leafy green salads a mandatory option. The calorie content of most meals is also being lowered. And even if you are a visitor, you will not be able to find a candy bar in a New York City hospital vending machine.

The Harvard Medical School in partnership with the Culinary Institute of America put on workshops titled "Healthy Kitchens/Healthy Lives." These hands-on cooking workshops are directed at doctors and other medical professionals to promote the kitchen as the center of a medical system for improving the health of society.

It's a simple idea, but the results will have a large impact. Since doctors are on the front line of the war on disease, they are best suited to spread the word about how healthy cooking and eating can change lives.

## Making changes

The incentive to make changes is strong. You have a 1 in 84 chance of dying in a car accident, a 1 in 7 chance of dying of cancer, and a 1 in 5 chance of dying of heart disease. And even if you don't succumb to heart disease, if enough plaque builds up, it may require a stent or bypass surgery. Bypass surgery is when surgeons crack open your rib cage and temporarily put your heart on an external pump, while they fix years of plaque build-up from years of reckless eating. Sensible eating seems much less painless.

The odds of dying in a car accident are much lower than dying from heart disease. But while many would not hesitate to spend more for a car with extra safety features to decrease the risk of dying in a car accident, very few of us make the effort to decrease the risk of cancer, heart disease, high blood pressure, Type II diabetes, and many other diseases.

My wife Carol has spent most of her career as a cardiac nurse. Just in that period of time, she has seen the average age of heart bypass patients decrease. It is now estimated that 1 out of every 20 people below the age of 40 has heart disease. Heart disease is the silent killer, where fatty substances narrow and eventually block the flow of blood to the heart. A sign that things may get worse is that the FDA has approved Lipitor (a cholesterol lowering medicine) for use in children as young as 10 years old. And Pravachol (another statin type drug) is approved for kids eight years old. What are we eating that children are on drugs for plaque buildup by their eighth birthday?

Making the changes that ensure a healthier life can take some effort. Most of us have favorite foods and recipes that we've enjoyed for many years. It takes some time to edit grocery lists and rework recipes. Food scientists say a lifetime of eating causes imprints on the brain, which are difficult to change. There may also be added pressure, if not everyone in one's family is on board with the new menu. And then there are the societal pressures, as we live in a predominately meat eating country with fast food ingrained into our lifestyles.

The diet changes that are made slowly are the ones that have the highest chance of success. Extreme changes, whether it is to how we eat, exercise or live, rarely work. (Though there is a minority of people who do thrive on the revolutionary, not evolutionary, way of changing things.) To this day, I still make subtle changes, as I read books and articles, talk to knowledgeable people, and try new foods. Three years ago, I had never heard of quinoa (a high protein grain from South America), but now I eat it twice a week.

Making a small change like adding an extra salad or two per week might be a good place to start. You can introduce new meatless products gradually, maybe in only a meal a week, at first. When temptation for something unhealthy strikes, it shouldn't be too hard to resist, as the motivation for eating well is a healthier body. Compromises are okay at the start, when the goal is making better food choices for a lifetime.

I often get asked if I think my diet was what really cured me. I wish it was that simple. Healthy food is powerful medicine, and my diet provided me with optimal nutrition at a time when my body was most vulnerable. This also had the effect of eliminating man-made additives with unknown health risks. It's hard to separate cause and effect, especially on one individual, but the end result is I lived far longer and with far fewer health issues than anyone thought possible. In short, it was a critical element in how I beat the odds. I also believe that some of the patients I befriended experienced poor outcomes, at least in part, because they were feeding their bodies junk, just at the time when their bodies needed nutrition the most.

However, good nutrition is only part of the plan, and by itself is not always enough. One of the nurses, who worked in the unit where I received transfusions, was diagnosed with cancer. She was only in her 30's. She declined all chemo treatments and instead treated herself with a very strict raw foods plant based diet, including some exotic herbs.

I marveled at her dedication to healthier living, but like many others, I wondered if she should also accept the chemo. She stayed with her diet, rejecting medical treatment. Eventually the cancer spread and she took chemo, but it was too late, and she passed away.

We will never know if she would have survived had she taken treatment from the time of diagnosis. I do know she fed her body all the nourishment it craved, and she was stronger for that.

Eating a nutritious whole foods plant based diet is for the healthy and the sick. Start now.

ERIC HODIES

# CHAPTER 7 ~ LIVE WITH HOPE

*"Our bodies communicate to us clearly and specifically, if we are willing to listen to them."*

*- Shakti Gawain, author*

In the beginning, I wasn't just hopeful I would beat this thing, I was sure of it. Call it unbridled optimism or naiveté, but that was how I felt. Two failed treatments and hundreds of units of blood later, and that optimism gave way to reality. Somehow, I found myself stuck on the wrong path, and it was only a matter of time before this disease would take my life. Yet I still stayed hopeful. It might seem that those two feelings can't coexist, but they can.

In 2005, when I had the brain hemorrhage and my outlook seemed especially dismal, I took what I thought were very practical steps. I wrote my

117

obituary, so as not to give Carol that task. I began renewing my magazine subscriptions for only one year at a time. And I wrote sealed letters of appreciation to my family members and one close friend should I pass.

I had a strong dislike of aplastic anemia (ok, I hated it) and how the disease robbed me of many things I used to enjoy. In spite of that feeling, I never sank into a gloomy funk, and I never had a "sky is falling" moment. I simply arrived at a calm understanding of the reality of my situation. I would fight as much as possible, while also begrudgingly accepting my fate.

Maybe it was a little too much of that matter-of-fact perspective, but I knew none of us live forever. Life is precarious. I just happened to draw the short straw and the end was getting here a little sooner than I had planned.

Even so, I never gave up hope. I was on supportive care, so there really wasn't one good medical reason to remain hopeful. I guess I was hopeful that if I lived long enough, there would be new cures for almost everything, including aplastic anemia. I used that explanation often in conversation, in order to divert the topic and speak of something more positive. And I always got excited when I read about a new medical advance in stem cell research. But I knew to rely on a future medical cure that wasn't even in clinical trials was a little unrealistic. Medically, I had no reason to feel positive.

I believe I remained hopeful largely for one reason. I loved life and didn't want to miss one second of it. For ten years, there was a burning desire within me to eliminate doctor appointments, hospital visits, and blood transfusions and get back to doing some of the things that I used to enjoy so much. That really was all I could think about. I fought hard not because I was scared of death, but because I loved life. I wanted to live a normal life doing normal things, and I wasn't interested in any other alternative.

It's a cliché, but every day is a precious gift. I don't want to get all dreamy and cosmic sounding, but that's the truth. I was only in my 40's and I had so much more I wanted to do. I didn't have a bucket list, and I wasn't looking for fireworks. For me, it's always been about all the little things in life. I just had more mountain trails to hike, more cups of really good coffee to drink, and more great times with family and friends to enjoy. That was more than enough reason to be hopeful.

Anyone who ever visited me during a transfusion probably noticed the two small stones I would always set down on the small table attached to my chair. One had the word "strength" etched into it, and the other one had the word "hope" etched into it. They were given to me by my dad. It was my tradition to do that on transfusion day. I love traditions. They may have been two silly little rocks, but they meant so much to me. With that word "hope" staring back at me, I had a lot to live up to. Get your own stones, and you will always have hope close by.

Children are hopeful by instinct. A cancer survivor once said, "If children have the ability to ignore all odds and percentages, then maybe we can all learn from them. When you think about it, what other choice is there but to hope? We have two options, medically and emotionally: give up, or Fight Like Hell." At every fork in the road on your journey, choose the later and do it with gusto.

Hope can come from within, and it can also come from others. I was lucky to have a strong support system of family and friends, and I know it helped keep me in good spirits. There is a lot of waiting around when you're sick, and it's a lifesaver to have diversions. Nothing would make my day more than to get a phone call or an email on my blood transfusion day.

Studies have confirmed that those people with the strongest social relationships tend to live healthier and longer lives. Social ties are so important that people with strong social relationships and unhealthy lifestyles tend to live longer than those with few social relationships but healthier lifestyles. That's some pretty powerful medicine.

I think there were times when a few of my friends were nervous about asking me how I was doing. Maybe they thought I didn't want to talk about my illness. Or maybe they didn't know what to ask. If you're ever nervous or in doubt, my advice is to always ask. Ask something, anything. Almost every time, you will make someone's day. Their illness is only the biggest thing going on in their life. On the occasion when someone doesn't feel like talking, they'll let you know.

My friends were the reason I had my Celebration of Life party in the summer of 2005. I was on supportive care, getting the blood to stay alive, and doing the best I could. I had just dodged a bullet, with my brain hemorrhage. I didn't feel an impending sense of doom, rather that things were just going in the wrong direction. The time was right for the Celebration of Life party.

The party gave me the opportunity to get all my friends together while I could still enjoy the day and thank everyone personally for their support. Dr. Alexander was one of my biggest advocates for having the celebration. From his perspective as an oncologist, he stressed the importance of saying thank-you while you still can and not putting it off until it was too late. I didn't want to make that mistake.

The Celebration of Life took place outside on a large,

wooden deck in the dunes overlooking the Atlantic Ocean on a picture perfect September day. One friend played music, and another friend read a piece of heartfelt inspiration he wrote just for the occasion. We ended the party with a colorful balloon release. We had tags available, so everyone could write a personal note or wish and attach it to a balloon. The support was heartening, and it made me feel close to everyone. I remember arriving home afterwards, thinking I was the luckiest man alive. Life was great, no matter what.

What I felt that day was a massive endorphin rush and boost to my spirit that few people ever get to experience. The source of it was simply the end result of an enormous outpouring of support from friends and family. Dr. Alexander states this power cannot be underestimated. The patients with the most support will have the most hope, and that hope is crucial in dealing with the disease process. He points out that those who do not find hope will feel lost and almost universally will have poorer outcomes.

Six years after that Celebration of Life party, the tables turned in a way I could not have expected. It was April of 2011, and my blood counts were slowly increasing and the time between transfusions was lengthening. I finally had reason to hope. When I informed friends and family of this amazing news, I was always at a shortage of words to describe how I felt.

I was equal parts relieved, shocked and grateful over this turn of events. I had day dreamed thousands of times of what it would feel like to get better. I knew it would be wonderful. But when it actually happened, I couldn't find the words to accurately describe what I was feeling. I was getting a second chance at life. How do you put something like that into words?

Then the other shoe dropped. My wife was diagnosed with breast cancer. It was hard to believe. I had been struck with a very rare blood disease and now my wife had to fight a very rare and aggressive growing cancer. The growth rate of her cancer was so high it was necrotic (the cancer was growing so fast that parts of it were dying before it could get nourishment). The biopsy revealed a cancer with a

Nottingham score of 9, the highest score possible, indicating maximum aggressiveness of the cancer. Hadn't we been through enough?

It didn't seem fair. Hadn't we had our share? We joked that our house must have been built on top of an old toxic waste dump. But maybe we were getting a lucky break. A break in that I was doing well, feeling better, and not spending much time in the hospital or at doctor appointments. I would be better able to support Carol through any possible surgery, chemo and radiation.

Carol approached her illness much the same way I did. She became an informed patient, using her hospital contacts to become as knowledgeable and prepared as possible. She ate right, exercised and kept a positive outlook. In the end, Carol's surgery went well and she has been cancer free for almost two years. I believe that the pro-active participation in our treatments and hopeful attitudes played a large role in our positive outcomes.

I would be remiss to discuss hope and not say a few words about faith. I'm not aware of how my fellow patients felt about faith, because I consider it personal and didn't feel comfortable chatting with others about it. I do know that living with a life threatening illness will make you think hard about your place in the world and other philosophical matters that I find next to impossible to put into words. I've also spent a lot of time thinking about how some very good things have happened (writing this book is probably one) that would not have occurred otherwise. The end result is that, although I did not pray regularly pre-illness, that has now changed. Now, I pray often, before bed, on walks or even in the car at stoplights. Whether I was getting a transfusion or getting chemo, I felt like God was there with me. That gave me great comfort.

Alas, no matter how hard we try, the glass isn't always half full. Hope naturally ebbs and flows as we fight illness and try to regain health. My last ten years has been somewhat like a wild roller coaster ride, full of ups, downs, and even a few loops thrown in for good measure. However, whether my coaster was on the way up or the way down, my thoughts stayed focused on what I could do next to help myself. It's hard not to be hopeful when you are busy working on improving your future.

Disease can be devastating and rob you of many things. But it can't rob you of choice. You always have a choice. You can choose to sink in the negativity of your illness or you can choose to take an active part in your health. Take the good with the bad, but always keeping your focus on the good.

As I write this chapter, my neighbor is in the middle of 44 radiation treatments for his prostate cancer. He's in good spirits knowing there is less cancer in his body each day, and he is one day closer to health. His wife told me the number 44 isn't important. They would be almost as happy if it were 144 treatments. When there is an end in sight, hope is easy to find.

Sometimes, even with the best attitude, hope can be elusive. It's ok to feel sorry for yourself for a few minutes each day. It's hard not to. But move on. Energy spent stewing in negative thoughts is energy that could be better spent exercising or being with friends. I think back to that phrase about how it takes twice as many muscles to make a frown as it does a smile.

I've seen too many patients in their hospital rooms, lights out, blinds drawn, and TV blaring. They were spending way more than their allotted "feeling sorry time." I wondered what they were thinking. Their doctors told them to expect to be sick, so maybe they were just living out their diagnosis.

Do not live out your diagnosis.

Many of these patients were able to sit in the lobby or walk the halls, but they never did. Why didn't they walk even a little bit? Perhaps they could have changed things if they had put their minds to it, but they didn't. They didn't have hope.

Always live with hope.

# CHAPTER 8 ~ CONCLUSION

*"Strength does not come from physical capacity. It comes from an indomitable will."*

*- Mahatma Gandhi*

I am alive for many reasons. More than anything else, I would not be here today if not for the compassion of blood donors. They selflessly give up their time and a piece of themselves to help others. They are my heroes. I urge everyone to give blood, if only once. You won't have to wonder if your charitable donation is well spent. I can guarantee it. The gift of your blood will save someone's life.

From time to time, much is made about the safety of our blood supply and the workers who protect it. I am living proof that the blood supply is exceedingly safe, which wasn't the case not very long ago. If you are anemic and your doctor advises a red cell transfusion, take the blood. You will feel so much better, and you can feel comfortable that it is extremely safe.

Advances in medicine continue to increase survivability and quality of life for all patients. Even in the ten years I was sick, I saw major advances. For instance, my iron chelation drug that required a continuous day long infusion was replaced with a much more tolerable and safer oral pill. That single advancement greatly increased the quality of my life and allowed me to lead a more normal life.

I'm thankful for blood transfusions, medi-ports, oral chelators, and all the other wonders of modern medicine. In Aristotle's era, it was thought that the head contained a cooling organ, not a brain. That is because by the time autopsies were performed, the liquid matter in the brain had dried up, leaving an empty cavity, with no proof that there was a brain. We sure have come a long way.

In spite of the great advances, living with a life threatening illness is tricky in many ways. It takes a positive attitude, of course, but also attributes such as patience, tenacity, and vigilance. Not to be left off that list is good old fashioned luck. It's been said you don't beat cancer; you just get lucky and survive it.

I recognize the role luck played in my illness. I made

getting better my number one job and worked diligently toward that goal. That made a difference. But I didn't survive just because I did something special. I survived because I did something special and I was lucky. There are many others who fought the good fight in the same manner as I did, but without success. Steve Jobs is a well-known example, but alas, pancreatic cancer is tough to beat. A personal example is my mom who lost her brave fight to cancer. In spite of everything we can do to change our odds, some things are out of our control.

Good fortune and luck were on my side when I became ill at the age of 41. That age seemed like the perfect intersection of wisdom and youth. If I had been older, age would have worked against me. If I had been younger, I wouldn't have had the patience and wisdom that comes with age.

It's an understatement to say luck was also on my side when I met and married Carol. Because of Carol, I was fortunate enough to receive my very own crash course in clinical nursing: no bulky textbook necessary, as I was the patient. The fact I am alive and writing this book is a testament to Carol's knowledge and ability as a nurse. Her nursing skills, sharp eye, and quick thinking saved my life several times. She showed me how to become an educated patient, navigate the medical system, and become my own advocate. And she never left my side. Carol's knowledge, skill, and compassion can be found on every page of this book.

It's great to be fortunate, but it was wisdom and maturity that allowed me to realize complaining wouldn't have helped my cause or made me healthy again. Complaining would have been downright petty given that there was always someone down the hospital corridor worse off than me. Meanwhile, any added stress would have weakened my immune system further.

With maturity, major decisions were manageable. I knew it was prudent to listen to everybody, yet always make my own decisions. When there are so many different voices (doctors, family members, and friends) in your ear, it can be hard to filter and digest the advice and wishes of everyone. I worked hard to create my own circle of experts and confidants who would help me chart my path. I was determined to not become a jellyfish floating along in the current.

Lacking a crystal ball, time after time, I dug down deep and made the best decision given the circumstances. Though it was important to have support, I only had to answer to myself. I knew how I wanted to live. Everything I saw and heard was filtered through my own set of values, tendencies, and aversion to risk. And no one knew my body better than me. Others would likely have made different decisions with the same information and set of circumstances.

I also realized my body did not betray me. In fact, my earlier healthy lifestyle allowed me opportunities that others did not have. I had the enthusiasm and energy to better my condition and my situation. I was always thinking one step ahead of where I was. I remained highly self-motivated and ever eager to do something constructive to help my cause.

You won't find a convenient manual for how to handle situations like a life threatening disease, so you have to make one up as you go along. It's like being told you have to come up with a new recipe and you're given ingredients that don't normally mix well together. Ingredients like frustration, patience, humor, anger, optimism, and anxiety. It's the yin and yang of life thrown together and thrown at you, all at once.

It wasn't always easy, but I found the coping strategy that worked for me. I respected what others were doing and tried to understand and learn from them. In return, I hope others learned from me. But some lessons are only learned the hard way. Living with a chronic illness is a learning process and probably one of the biggest learning experiences any of us will ever face.

Was there an upside to my journey? You bet. No

ERIC HODIES

one wants to get sick with a life threatening illness
and suffer the physical and emotional stress that
comes with it, but you hear people say it's the best
thing that ever happened to them. I think that's
because pain and suffering can become useful tools.
To endure illness and regain our health, we must all
blaze our own path and fight as best we can. You
discover a lot about yourself while traveling that path.

Aplastic anemia became a learning tool. It allowed
me the opportunity to see first-hand the swiftness and
fragility of life. Aplastic anemia also left me with a
better understanding of what is important and what is
not. I wish everyone could feel what I did, if only for
a day. My personal take is that although success,
whether in career or athletics or anything else, is
important, it is secondary to the relationships we have
with family and friends. It is those relationships we
build and maintain through-out life that provide the
most comfort and support. Without those, we have
nothing.

I also learned that anything is possible. I'm referring
to my medical miracle, of course, but it applies to
many other things in life. I advise keeping an open
mind, even at what seems unlikely or goes against
your natural tendencies. Break free from
preconceived notions. If you do, the possibilities are
endless. If you don't, then you will only believe what
you have always believed. I walk away from my

illness having learned something valuable that will stay with me for life: On the way to making my own decisions, I will never discount a thought or idea just because it seems hard to believe or miraculous.

Another lesson I learned is how unforgiving the stark reality of illness can be. It's the ace that trumps all other cards. You can always change your job or move to another house. But a diagnosis is harsh, nonnegotiable, and inflexible. It comes with its own boundaries, rules, and timelines. And I found it best to learn those rules and respect them, though I never stopped pushing those boundaries

It's great to hear of others doing the same. I'll never forget the story of a local woman who was written up in the newspaper. She had been told she only had a 2% chance to live. Her response, upon hearing that only 2 out of a hundred would live, was "That's twice as much chance as I need!" What a great attitude.

From day one, it takes constant and never ending work to keep that attitude. It's remarkable how your perspective on life can change so quickly after diagnosis. It only takes a few numbers from a lab print out or the diagnosis your doctor scribbles on your chart to change your life. In a split second, life becomes clearer and simpler.

When you are lying in that hospital bed wondering when and if you will go home, you become very conscious of yourself. You uncover what you are made of, and what is truly important in your life. Once my diagnosis and its significance sank in, friends and family became more important, music sounded better, and nature looked more amazing.

I can't think of anything worse than losing your health. It will get your attention, and it will rattle you. I remember being told how long I could expect to live. It's not something that you think you will ever hear. At that point, my biggest opponent was not my disease, but fear of my disease. I couldn't be that deer in the headlights. There was a fork in the road, and I had to quickly choose one path over the other.

Always choose the path of health. Go ahead and make those changes today that will benefit you the rest of your life. You have the ability to manage your own health and wellness. Visualize what you want and then go after it. Instead of being a passive passenger, take action. It's not until you're threatened with losing what is most precious, that you develop a deep appreciation for your loved ones and for all that is taken for granted.

This life altering experience, as difficult as it was, has made me stronger, wiser, and more understanding and an overall better human being. I would not be the person I am today without having faced aplastic anemia. For that, I am grateful.

# APPENDIX

## ADDITIONAL READING AND VIEWING

<u>Healthy Eating</u>

Movies:

- ❖ 'Food Inc'
- ❖ 'Food Matters'
- ❖ 'King Corn'

Books:

- ❖ 'Crazy, Sexy Diet' by Kris Carr
- ❖ 'In Defense of Food:  An Eater's Manifesto' by Michael Pollan

## Mind-Body Connection

Book:

- ❖ 'Sunny Brain, Rainy Brain' by Dr. Elaine Fox

## Exercise

Book:

- ❖ 'The First 20 Minutes: Surprising Science Reveals How We Can: Exercise Better, Train Smarter, Live Longer' by Gretchen Reynolds

## Hope

Books:

- ❖ 'Tuesdays with Morrie: An Old Man, a Young Man, and Life's Greatest Lesson' by Mitch Albom
- ❖ 'Papillon' by Henri Charriere

*Note:* 'Papillon' was probably the most memorable book I read during my illness. It's the story of one man's relentless fight against overwhelming odds to regain his freedom. It was the very last item I tossed in our car as we were leaving for our two months at Johns Hopkins. I read it as a kid and reread it during my chemo. It was entertaining, inspiring and gave me hope.

*Article from* The Virginian Pilot, *reprinted with permission*
Publication Date: October 13, 2003
Section: Hampton Roads
Page: 1

Eric Hodies, a 42-year-old veteran of duathlons and triathlons, jogs toward the finish line of his 21st Sandman Triathlon on the    Virginia Beach Boardwalk. Hodies suffers from aplastic anemia, a condition in which his bone marrow cannot produce enough blood.

# He keeps running for his life

Despite his illness,
Va. Beach triathlete
stays in the race

BY DANIELLE R. ROACH
THE VIRGINIAN-PILOT

Eric Hodies begins
the running part of
the Sandman
Triathlon relay after
a hand from Donna
Harper, who did the
swimming portion
of the event.

VIRGINIA BEACH — For the past three months, Eric Hodies has trained nearly every day for the Sandman Triathlon, just as he has for the previous 20 Sandmans.

But this year was different. He trained as if his life depended on it. In many ways, it does.

Hodies wasn't fighting for the best time or the strongest swim. He's fighting for his life.

Hodies has aplastic anemia, a rare disease of the bone marrow in which the marrow stops making enough healthy blood cells.

That's why, over the past few months, he has walked anywhere from a few yards to a few miles, around his Virginia Beach home, around First Landing State Park, wherever.

For a man who is used to running, hiking, biking, and swimming with little effort, it may not sound like much. But to Hodies, it's everything.

"In July, I knew I'd be here," said Hodies, before launching his 5k journey, his wife, Carol, at his side. "I knew I'd have to train and build up to it, but I knew I'd make it."

Back then, it would have been a hard sell. After living with aplastic anemia for nearly eight months, Hodies was undergoing his second round of chemotherapy. It was part of a radical research study at Johns Hopkins University, a high-dose chemo, designed to restore blood cells by regenerating the bone marrow.

It will be several months before his doctors know if the treatment worked.

"The waiting is worse than the treatment," he said, in an honest but almost humor-filled tone. "I'm just waiting to see if my blood cell count goes up. If it works, it works, if not, well, I don't like to think about the other."

So, for the past few months, he has focused less on the possibility of dying and more on living a life that resembles, at least in some ways, the one he left behind last Christmas Eve, when he was diagnosed.

"He's just accepted it and tries to move on, and he's so positive about everything," said his wife. "He finds the best in all the changes, taking in everything he can in his new life."

On Sunday, that included piecing together a relay team, with friends doing the biking and swimming legs of the race, and Hodies crossing the finish line after the 5k. The bike race was canceled in the wake of Hurricane Isabel, so that left only the swim and run/walk.

Over the past two decades, the swimming portion of the race had been Eric's favorite, but on Sunday, he gladly relied on long-time friend Donna Harper.

As Harper rushed out of the water, she tagged Eric and his wife to start their trek, and the tears flowed for all three.

"That water was brutal, it was tough," Harper said. "But I kept thinking about him and what he goes through every single day. I knew it might take me a while, but if he can do this, then I can do this."

Together, they did.

About an hour later, Hodies broke into a steady jog for the final 50 yards. The crowd erupted into cheers of "Go, Eric."

"This really meant so much to me," said Hodies, 42, after crossing the finish line. "For that hour, we didn't talk about my illness at all, and it felt like old times, like nothing had changed."

*Continued* 'Running'...

138

Eric Hodies walks with his wife, Carol, toward the finish line at the Neptune Festival's Sandman Triathlon before breaking into a jog for the last 50 yards. Hodie suffers from aplastic anemia, a bone marrow disorder.

# Running: Disease, therapy didn't stop him

**On the surface,** little has changed. He still looks the part of an athlete, a tan, chiseled face, a confident, contagious smile, with legs as strong as his spirit.

It's hard to notice the catheter running to his heart, which he flushes every day, or the red dots on his legs — bursting capillaries from the lack of a blood-clotting mechanism.

Unless you knew him before his diagnosis, it's even hard to recognize his baldness as a side effect of the chemo or just the preference of a guy who could wear just about anything, and wear it well.

It's hard to notice, but for Eric, it's just as hard to forget.

"I think about the catheter and all the blood transfusions, but I don't dwell on it," he said.

Hodies has received more than 60 transfusions, averaging one every few weeks. In essence, he's relying on the kindness of strangers, from blood and platelet donations to stacks of get-well cards.

On Sunday, that generosity took on a new form — money. This year's participants could make a contribution in Eric's name or raise money through donations for aplastic anemia research at Johns Hopkins Medical Center, said Brian Sagedy, the race director.

About $3,000 was raised by the 450 participants.

But for Hodies, it was well worth the wait.

"It's so nice just to be out here, to be a part of it," he said. "I've got to make the most of it. I mean, who knows, I might be in this same situation next year."

For now, he's going to keep living by the same philosophy as his hero, Lance Armstrong.

"I can't die if I don't stop moving."

Nani Tosoc, right, ran in the event wearing a T-shirt in support of Eric Hodies, left. Participants raised about $3,000 in Hodies' honor for research of aplastic anemia.

■ *Reach Danielle R. Roach*
*446-2536*
danielle.roach@pilotonline.com

*Online article from* The Aplastic Anemia and MDS International Foundation, *reprinted with permission*
  Publication Date: July 12, 2012 (Updated July13, 2012)
  URL: http://www.aamds.org/node/1254

# Eric Hodies – A Study in Attitude and Self-Advocacy

### The Diagnosis

In 2002, 41-year-old Eric Hodies was a devoted triathlete, training for his 21st Virginia Beach Sandman Triathlon. He had competed in the event every year since its inception, and he was looking forward to another great race. But in the months leading up to the event, he noticed that he was getting slower and slower, despite the fact that he was increasing the intensity of his workouts. Ever attune to the signals his body was sending him, he went to a doctor. He was initially diagnosed with asthma, but further tests revealed that it was aplastic anemia.

"My workouts saved my life," says Eric. "We were planning to go out on a long hiking trip in the wilderness the day after I was diagnosed, so it was a very good thing that I was working out and found out when I did."

### Treatment Attempts

Eric never questioned why the illness struck him. All

of his energy was focused on getting better. Formerly an engineer, he says, "Aplastic anemia is a great disease to have if you're an engineer. It's all about numbers and your counts. There are a lot of numbers, so it's kind of a good thing to be an engineer. We're problem solvers."

He's also a strong proponent of self-education. Within hours of his diagnosis, he had read just about everything he could find about aplastic anemia on the internet, including information from AA&MDSIF and a clinical trial website. He says, "even if you don't understand every little detail, you can use common sense to figure out the gist of things."

Unfortunately, the primary treatment for aplastic anemia, ATG (anti-thymocyte globulin) was ineffective for Eric. He then tried high-dose cytoxan chemotherapy at the Johns Hopkins Hospital. This treatment also proved ineffective, though it took a year of waiting to know for sure that he had not responded to it.

Because neither treatment resulted in remission, Eric has had low blood counts for more than eight years. He has relied on transfusions of more than 800 units of blood in that time, getting a transfusion every 8-10 days. He describes his situation as a unique case – he's just gone on living with aplastic anemia. Over time, his body has adapted to low blood counts, and he gets a transfusion whenever his hemoglobin drops to 8 (half of normal). As a result, he always feels tired and naps regularly.

**Life with Aplastic Anemia**

It has been an adjustment. Before, he'd work out every single day. He says of that time, "I couldn't even imagine being sick. I never got sick. If you had asked me the day before I was diagnosed, I thought I was going to live to 1000. When I went in, I thought they were just going to wave a wand and I'd be back on my feet in no time."

Eric has also stopped working. Though his boss was really fantastic about the situation, Eric felt he couldn't keep his job with the frequent doctor appointments and transfusions, not to mention the general fatigue. He was led to believe that he didn't have much time left, and he didn't want to spend his remaining days at work. Nonetheless, leaving his career was not an easy decision. He remembers crying, partially because leaving work seemed to represent going home to die.

There are other aspects of his life that have been affected as well: "There's not been a day when my wife and I haven't talked about the disease in eight years. We always talk about the next appointment, getting blood, the [Hickman] catheter; there's always a lot to discuss. It affects us, but not a lot. I've grown to accept it."

## Living Well

Despite numerous setbacks, including a hemorrhagic stroke in 2005 and another life-threatening situation in which his catheter broke, Eric has never given up. He believes in three primary approaches to staying well: 1) a positive attitude, 2) daily exercise, and 3) nutrition. "I don't believe in a magic pill," he says. "We eat really healthy food. It's not the whole answer, but it's one part of the puzzle."

He also relies on the help of his wife and his medical team. He says, "Nurses at the hospital are my friends. I know them, we talk, and they know me. I know half the people in the hospital. My doctor and I see eye-to-eye. I've been very lucky, but I've also worked very hard to assemble a great team."

## Challenges

The hardest part for Eric in dealing with the medical profession has been insurance issues. His medical bills in the first year came to nearly $1 million including hospitalizations, renting an apartment during his treatment at Johns Hopkins, blood transfusions, and chelation therapy. He was initially denied one expensive chelator that was designed specifically for people with similar histories of extensive transfusions. His ferritin (iron level) was at 5700 at that point. Without treatment, that level of iron could have caused organ damage. His doctor was finally able to get it approved by talking to the insurance company doctor.

"My experience is that if you call up the insurance company and talk about what they're denying, and if you fight it, they'll say yes. But they deny everything initially. I call them right away. That's part of my job now. My job is to stay healthy, and keeping insurance straight is part of that."

## Advice for Survival

Eric recommends that anyone who is seriously ill needs to surround themselves with the best medical professionals they can. He says to never give up until you find the right people: "You have to be happy with your team.

You have to be a little aggressive. You have to be willing to find another doctor [if you don't agree with the first one]. You have to be your own advocate. If you're not happy, you just have to keep going." Eric notes that every doctor is offering the right advice to somebody, so it's just a matter of being patient as you find the right one for you. He says, "This is my body and I have to take responsibility."

Part of finding the right team includes educating yourself. Eric was the one who found the treatments he underwent. "You need to get on-line – there's tons of great information out there. Start at the AA&MDSIF website. I even e-mail doctors who write articles in journals. Get two or three opinions right off the bat and discuss them – with someone who has good ears. Aplastic anemia is not a clear case. There are a lot of decisions and a lot of different treatments to choose from. Learn about yourself."

144

## Winning the Race

Exercise has Eric's saved life, along with a powerfully positive attitude and never-waning desire to continue his race all the way to the finish. With the help of a team, Eric competed in and finished the 21st Sandman Triathlon, a true testament to his determination and positive attitude. He is practically brimming with positive affirmations. He says, "I've always appreciated life, but more so now."

These days, he's running the race of his life, and despite the fantastic hurtles in his way, he's winning.

---

The Aplastic Anemia and MDS International Foundation

(800) 747-2820
(301) 279-7202

100 Park Avenue
Suite 108
Rockville, Maryland
20850 U.S.A.

www.aamds.org

## Update – July 13, 2012:

It appears Eric has won his battle. Since this article was written, he has gone into spontaneous remission without any treatments or medications. He is now transfusion free and his counts continue to increase. Last month, his port catheter was finally removed after nine years.

"My hematologist agrees with calling it a miracle," says Eric. "I am at work writing a book to document my last ten years of aplastic anemia."

We can't wait to read it!

ERIC HODIES

Made in the USA
Lexington, KY
17 February 2013